REFUGEES

ASYLUM
IN EUROPE?

Minority Rights Publications

Minority Rights Group is an international, non-governmental organization whose aims are to ensure justice for minority (and non-dominant majority) groups suffering discrimination by:

1. Researching and publishing the facts as widely as possible to raise public knowledge and awareness of minority issues worldwide.

2. Advocating on all aspects of human rights of minorities to aid the prevention of dangerous and destructive conflicts.

3. Educating through its schools programme on issues relating to prejudice, discrimination and group conflicts.

If you would like to know more about the work of the Minority Rights Group, please contact Alan Phillips (Director), MRG, 379 Brixton Road, London SW9 7DE, United Kingdom.

𝓶

Minority Rights Publications is a new series of books from the Minority Rights Group. Through the series, we aim to make available to a wide audience reliable data on, and objective analyses of, specific minority issues. The series draws on the expertise and authority built up by the Minority Rights Group over two decades of publishing. Further details on MRG's highly acclaimed series of reports can be found at the end of this book. Other titles in the book series are:

The Balkans: Minorities and States in Conflict
by Hugh Poulton (1991)

Armenia and Karabagh: The Struggle for Unity
Edited by Christopher J. Walker

The Kurds: A Nation Denied
by David McDowall

REFUGEES

ASYLUM IN EUROPE?

by
Daniéle Joly

with
Clive Nettleton
and Hugh Poulton

Foreword by
Ian Martin

Minority Rights Publications

© Minority Rights Group 1992

First published in Great Britain
in 1992 by
Minority Rights Publications
379 Brixton Road
London SW9 7DE

British Library Cataloguing in Publication Data
A CIP catalogue record of this book is available from the British Library.

ISBN 1 873194 10 2 paper
ISBN 1 873194 35 8 hardback

Library of Congress Cataloguing in Publication Data
CIP Data available from the Library of Congress

Designed and typeset by Brixton Graphics
Printed and bound by Billing and Sons Ltd

Cover photo of asylum seekers from Turkey in Germany/
UNHCR

CONTENTS

FOREWORD

by Ian Martin

Safeguarding the right to seek asylum must be very high on the overall agenda of those committed to the protection of human rights, and safeguarding the rights of minorities must be equally important for those who are concerned to prevent people being compelled to flee their countries and seek asylum elsewhere.

The answer to repression is not, of course, to transfer whole populations at risk to countries where there is a greater freedom and respect for human rights: it is to promote the protection of human rights, including the rights of minorities, in all countries. The publications of Minority Rights Group International have made an important contribution towards this objective.

Nevertheless the Universal Declaration of Human Rights proclaims for everyone 'the right to seek and to enjoy in other countries asylum from persecution'. While grave human rights violations persist in so many countries, international law, as well as simple humanity, prohibits states from sending any asylum-seeker back to a country where he or she is at risk of persecution or abuse.

Governments, however, are more often motivated by self-interest than by considerations of humanity, and this provides a further reason for those seeking to combat human rights violations to insist upon the right of asylum. States are keen to protect themselves from a refugee influx, even when it is the clear consequence of repression. Safeguarding the right to seek asylum will thus not only protect the people at risk in the short-term, but will harness the self-interest of states so that attention is focused on the conditions which led to their flight. If, after 1933, the states of Europe had been forced to recognize that persecuted German Jews were entitled to asylum and protection, would the same states have been so slow to condemn Nazi tyranny?

In the summer of 1992, it is impossible to read the proofs of this book without constant reference to the brutal war in the former Yugoslavia, the forcible expulsions in the context of 'ethnic cleansing' campaigns, the millions of displaced people, and the petty squabbling over refugee quotas among Western European governments. For the first time, the book presents a Europe-wide view of refugee issues, adding an excellent discussion of population movements and asylum issues in Eastern Europe to a broad examination of all aspects of refugee treatment in Western European states.

Although credit is given throughout to the positive aspects of government policy towards asylum-seekers and refugees, and to the work of governmental and non-governmental agencies, the overall picture is one that should shame Europeans. In other regions of the world, poorer countries afford asylum to far greater numbers : Bangladesh to upwards of 300,000 Muslims fleeing persecution in Myanmar (Burma); Kenya to half a million people displaced by the conflicts in Somalia, Sudan and Ethiopia; Iran to thousands of Kurds from the north and Shia from the south of Iraq, in addition to over two million Afghan refugees.

Meanwhile, the governments of Western Europe introduce measures to prevent victims of persecution from even reaching their borders to seek asylum, collaborate in secrecy to apply more restrictively their asylum procedures, and claim that they are motivated by the long-term interests of refugees when they discuss 'solutions' which leave the refugees on or near the territories the refugees are fleeing, while being unresponsive to urgent pleas to share in meeting the immediate needs for even short-term asylum. Many Western European politicians, together with much of its press, combine occasional displays of sympathy for refugees with a more consistent willingness to evoke racist sentiments for electoral advantage, by exaggerating abuse of the asylum process and by portraying asylum-seekers as part of the 'threat' of alien immigration.

The wheel has come full circle : from international agreements emerging from a European crisis at the end of the World War II; through a period when large outflows of refugees seemed to be a phenomenon of the South, far away from the borders of Europe; to a new European crisis of the 1990s. Western Europe condemns the 'ethnic cleansing' to which the reawakened nationalisms of Eastern Europe have given rise. Will either part of Europe rise above the irrational fear of minorities and the political temptation to exploit ethnic and political conflicts, which is reflected in and endorsed by a restrictive approach to refugees?

Ian Martin

Ian Martin was Secretary General of Amnesty International from 1986 to September 1992. Among the other posts he has previously held, he served as General Secretary of the Joint Council for the Welfare of Immigrants from 1977 to 1982.

Acknowledgements

This book is based on *Refugees in Europe* (MRG Report, 1990), revised, extended and updated to cover events and legislation up till mid-May 1992. The majority of the book was written by Daniéle Joly with some assistance from Clive Nettleton, who also helped with the diagrams and tables. Chapters 10, 11, 12 and 13 on refugees in Eastern Europe were written especially for this book by Hugh Poulton. The Introduction and Conclusions were written by MRG after consultation with the authors.

The detailed situation of refugees in Europe is constantly changing and, in some cases, a decree of secrecy surrounds current forthcoming practice or legislation; it is therefore inevitable that some material may not be current at the time of publication. However, as far as it is able, MRG has ensured that all information is current as of mid-May 1992. In the ensuing months the situation of refugees and displaced people in the former Yugoslavia worsened considerably.

MRG extends special thanks to Philip Rudge and the staff of the European Consultation on Refugees and Exiles (ECRE) for their patient assistance with factual information and interpretation.

MRG gratefully thanks Ian Martin for writing the Foreword to this book.

This book was produced by Kaye Stearman (Series Editor), Brian Morrison (Production Co-ordinator), Gloria Mitchell (Editorial Assistant), Robert Webb (Publicity and Marketing).

About the authors

Dr Daniéle Joly was born in France and attended universities at Nanterre and La Sorbonne (France) and Aston (UK). She is currently Senior Research Fellow of the Centre for Research in Ethnic Relations (CRER) in the University of Warwick. She has written and edited many articles and books, individually and with others, on immigration, Muslims in the UK and refugees in Europe. Her most recent book is *The French Communist Party and the Algerian War* (1991). She wishes to give special thanks to Gustavo Jara for his invaluable support during the writing of this book and to Nicolas Jara for the inspiration he provided.

Clive Nettleton came to the UK as a refugee in 1979 and has since worked extensively with refugees, both in the World University Service and the British Refugee Council in London where he was Head of Information, working in research, evaluation and information. He has published widely on refugee issues. He is currently Director of Health Unlimited, a development organization working in areas of conflict.

Hugh Poulton is a specialist in human rights in Eastern Europe who has travelled extensively in the region. His publications for the Minority Rights Group include: *Minorities in the Balkans* (MRG Report, 1989); *Romania's Ethnic Hungarians* (with George Schöpflin, MRG Report, 1990); and *The Balkans: Minorities and States in Conflict* (Minority Rights Publications, 1991).

INTRODUCTION

Images of violence and destruction – the indiscriminate shelling of towns and villages, the killing of unarmed civilians, the use of hunger as a weapons against whole populations – appear daily on television screens. Every day of every week, somewhere in the world, the victims of these conflicts are forced to flee in an attempt to reach safety. Frequently, the only escape will be to leave and seek asylum in another country.

Until recently, Europe could watch these images – from Vietnam, Sri Lanka, Ethiopia, Kurdistan and many more – with the detachment of distance. Today the development of a worldwide communications network via satellite means that horrific events can be transmitted almost instantaneously via television broadcasts and radio transmissions while in-depth accounts can appear in the next days' newspapers.

These images of unremitting and extreme violence were so regular that demands for relief for the victims became a constant accompaniment. Yet these appeals seemed to make little real difference. A new phase 'compassion fatigue' was coined to describe public reaction. Many western governments were complacent, indifferent or cynical; their policies towards individual countries were shaped by the superpower rivalry and the potential political advantage to each. Human rights considerations were immaterial or, if they were considered, were used as a political leverage or as a public relations tool.

Today, for European governments at least, it is difficult to remain complacent. Violence and destruction is occurring within Europe, as the Yugoslav state is destroyed and hundreds of thousands of people flee in terror from the fighting. Europeans are reminded that the end of the Cold War and of super-power rivalry will not automatically usher in an era of peace or prosperity. Many of the actual or latent conflicts, often exploited in the last period of Communist governments in their attempts to divide and rule, revolve around attempts to exacerbate tensions between the majority community and ethnic or linguistic minorities. There are disturbing indicators that new conflicts, producing new refugee flows, are likely to erupt.

1

In these circumstances it is essential to examine much more closely than hitherto what can be done to tackle the root causes of these conflicts before they lead to violence. The independent scholars and organizations like the Minority Rights Group have undertaken considerable work in investigating the specific circumstances in which repressive, undemocratic or complacent governments ignore minority grievances, allowing resentments to fester, leading to tensions and, sometimes, violence. The Minority Rights Group believes strongly that the granting of minority rights is an important factor in the creation of peaceful coexistence within states and between states.

Important although these ideas are, they are not the theme of this book, which deals with the consequences rather than the causes of conflict. It examines, in considerable detail, the policies and practices used in Europe to respond to those who seek asylum, not only of the ways in which asylum-seekers can seek refuge in Europe, but also of reception and settlement policies and programmes. All of these aspects are especially important given the great increase in the numbers of asylum-seekers in the past decade.

It is clear that as Western European states attempt to move towards greater economic and political union, including facilitating the mobility of people within the European Community, inconsistencies in policies have major implications for other European states. The key word for this process is 'harmonization', a word which has taken a different meaning in different contexts. Non-Government Organizations (NGOs) have taken the lead in expressing a concern that while 'harmonization' appears to be leading to much greater stringency in entry policies, it rarely leads to states learning from each other on how to invest effectively in good reception and settlement programmes for refugees.

As international travel becomes easier, asylum-seekers see Europe as a more accessible place of refuge. There may be some debate on where refugees seek asylum, for example whether they could have found sanctuary in a neighbouring country, as indeed the vast majority of refugees do, but it should be remembered that, even with the present increased numbers of asylum-seekers, Europe receives only a small proportion of the world's refugees. Furthermore, even a simple inspection of the country of origin of many of Europe's asylum-seekers (eg. Turkey, Iraq, Iran, Sri Lanka, Somalia) reveals that, by any standards these are countries where there have been major violent conflicts or gross human rights abuse.

It is important to remember the fundamental difference between the 20 million migrant workers, presently calculated to be in Western

Europe, and the one million refugees. Migrants can choose where, when and how they leave their country, asylum-seekers cannot. It is ironic that at a time that officials from European ministries of the interior are regularly meeting to explore ways of restricting access of refugees into Europe, other officials from ministries of employment and labour are investigating ways of overcoming a forthcoming anticipated shortage of labour at the end of the century, by increasing the numbers of migrant workers in Europe.

The question of migration takes an added impetus with the worsening economic situation in Eastern Europe and the Commonwealth of Independent States. In the past, when the numbers of asylum-seekers from the region were relatively low and evidence of individual persecution was strong, there were few problems in recognizing them as refugees. Today, the regimes and the circumstances have changed. Individual persecution is less likely but, in some areas, indiscriminate violence against members of some ethnic groups, such as the Roma, has increased while everywhere unemployment and poverty has deepened. Appropriate and humane long and short-term measures need to be developed.

The book avoids taking simple value judgements, for there are no simple ways forward. It is easy to blame government officials but they are bound by financial and political restrictions and frequently lack accurate information or specialist training. This book may be a resource for those who have to design and implement policies and who wish to learn from the experiences of others in order to develop better policies and practices.

But there is an urgent need for more dynamic leadership to confront racism and prejudice and to invest resources in refugees to enable them to be full members of society. An open constructive debate is needed involving the public, NGOs, government officials and elected politicians. This may not result in consensus but more civilized and humane policies should emerge.

3

4

1

MASS MOVEMENTS –
THE NEED FOR AN INTERNATIONAL
REFUGEE SYSTEM

'First they came for the Jews and I did not speak out -
  because I was not a Jew.
Then they came for the communists and I did not speak out -
  because I was not a communist.
Then they came for the trade unionists and I did not speak out -
  because I was not a trade unionist.
Then they came for me - and there was no one left to speak out for me.'

– Attributed to Pastor Niemoeller (victim of the Nazis).

Although mass exoduses have existed since ancient times, it is only in the 20th Century that refugee movements have become an international political issue requiring international legal instruments and political agreements as the framework for their solution.

There have been attempts to document and analyze the causes of modern refugee movements. Marrus[1] notes three distinguishing factors. Firstly, there was the dramatic rise in refugee numbers. Secondly, the movements were accompanied by a radically new form of homelessness. As nation-states took over the civil functions formerly provided by the Church and local communities, refugees became increasingly marginalized:

'Outside the state from which they had come, refugees could not work, could not live, could not live unmolested, could usually not remain at liberty for any length of time... modern refugees... differed from those of earlier times because their homelessness removed them so dramatically and uniquely from civil society'.

An earlier scholar, Hope-Simpson, remarked in 1939 that:

5

'The whole system (of nationality) is based on a scheme of national states, with populations which fit into the scheme of nationalities. The person without a nationality, and without the protection of their national representatives does not fit into that system.'[2]

Finally, the duration of exile increased and refugee camps became common as attempts were made to find solutions to the problems this growing class of uprooted people presented their often reluctant hosts.[3]

Dissolution of the old order

But if it was the formation of the new nation-states that made life so difficult for refugees, it was the dissolution of the old Europe and the bloody birth of the modern era that lay at the root of the growing crisis. The number of people displaced across international boundaries in the four years of World War I were equal to the numbers who moved in the 20 years following it. After the war, many of those who had moved – Belgians, Serbs, Poles, Lithuanians, Russians – returned to their homes.[4] But there were large numbers who did not, and many refugees were rendered stateless as new nations and new borders were established. Jewish refugees, in particular, found themselves without a state which would claim them.[5]

As the old order collapsed the refugee numbers grew rapidly, and the need for mechanisms to deal with their plight became more urgent. In the Balkans World War I finally completed the long disintegration of the Ottoman Empire. With its multiplicity of ethnic, linguistic and religious groups, each seeking to establish its claim to a national territory, conflicts were extremely violent and refugees fled ever more horrific massacres. Assyrians, Armenians, Chaldeans, Jews, Turks, Serbs and Macedonians fled from the advances of each other's armies.[6]

Birth of an international system

It was, finally, the Russian Revolution of 1917 and its aftermath that led to the establishment of an international system to deal with the refugee problem. Over a million refugees fled over the changing Soviet borders between 1917 and 1921.[7] While non-governmental organizations had provided assistance and relief to refugees, these were not sufficient to address the problems. Governments *'had to find ways of working together to address refugee and displaced persons problems that outstripped the capacity of individual states.'8*

In 1921 Fridtjof Nansen was appointed by the League of Nations as 'High Commissioner on Behalf of the League in connection with the Problem of Russian Refugees in Europe'. A Norwegian explorer of almost legendary status, Nansen had been involved in a private capacity in negotiating the repatriation of Russian and Austro-Hungarian prisoners of war.[9] His appointment marked the emergence of the first formal attempt to establish an international system to deal with refugee issues. Support, however, was tentative: Nansen was given only administrative support by the League; non-governmental organizations provided the personnel and supplies needed for assistance.

Nansen's preferred option was to seek the repatriation of refugees, but he was clear in asserting that this should be voluntary, thus establishing a principle that was to become central to refugee law and practice.[10] Many refugees, however, did not want to return, and both they and the political opponents of the new Soviet regime ensured that refugees were allowed either to remain in the countries to which they had fled or to be resettled elsewhere.

To enable refugees to move on in an age in which nationality had become increasingly important, documentation was required. Many of the refugees were stateless and a travel document, the 'Nansen passport', was awarded to specific national groups who had lost the protection of their state of origin: to Russian refugees (in 1922), Armenians (in 1924), Assyrians, Assyro-Chaldeans, Syrians, Kurds and Turks (all in 1928).

World War II and its aftermath

Events leading up to, during and immediately following World War II brought about a radical rethinking of the international structures for dealing with refugees. In the 1930s, specific national groups, including refugees from Germany (1936 and 1938) and Sudeten refugees from Czechoslovakia (1939) were able to benefit from international conventions and resolutions.[11] But:

'the real story and tragedy of this period is not those refugees that fled their countries and were not helped, but those that remained behind for a variety of reasons.'12

These included individual Russians and other Soviet citizens unable to escape Stalin's purges of the 1930s and, most dramatically, the survivors of the Holocaust.

Although the League of Nations had established a 'High Commission for Refugees (Jewish and other) coming from Germany' in 1933, it had been unable to provide protection for those who were trying to escape. The first High Commissioner, James G. McDonald, resigned in December 1935 in protest against his inability to deal effectively with the situation.[13] In his letter of resignation McDonald argued that it was not sufficient to attempt to alleviate the circumstances of people who had fled: political action was required to address the causes.[14] Jews seeking to leave Germany were prevented from doing so because they had to leave behind their financial assets. At a time of economic depression they were unable to fulfil the condition of potential host countries that they should not become a burden on the public purse.

It was on this dichotomy that the Evian Conference called by President Roosevelt in mid-1938 foundered. The UK blocked the possibility of resettlement in Palestine which it administered under a League of Nations mandate. The conference established the Inter-governmental Committee on Refugees which was mandated, but failed, to negotiate an orderly process of migration.[15]

In the face of the international community's failure to provide a solution, increasing numbers of Jews fled Germany in spite of the dangers and the lack of certainty on the other side of the border. By the outbreak of war in 1939 there were an estimated 100,000, mainly Jewish, refugees in Europe who had not been resettled.[16]

As the war progressed, the number of refugees and displaced people swelled to an unprecedented flood. One estimate[17] is that 60 million civilians were forced to move from their homes. Many thousands of refugees did manage to escape, but it was the Holocaust that convinced the international community, and particularly the European and American governments, of the urgent need to find a way forward.

In the immediate aftermath of the war the Allies were faced with the immense task of finding a secure home for millions of displaced people and refugees. The United Nations Relief and Rehabilitation Agency (UNRRA) was set up with their resettlement as its main objective. Its task was made even more complicated by the expulsion of over 12 million ethnic Germans from the areas of Eastern Europe occupied by Soviet forces.[18] By 1947 when the UNRRA was replaced by the International Refugee Organization (IRO) there were still over a million refugees in Europe.[19]

Working outside the UN system, the IRO focused primarily on resettlement. With the post-war economic recovery demanding more work-ers, the organization was highly successful in its task. But as the years passed, new crises, particularly in Eastern Europe indicated that European refugees were not going to disappear. In December 1950, as the IRO mandate expired, the Office of the United Nations High Commissioner for Refugees (UNHCR) was established, with the first High Commissioner taking office on 1 January 1951. On 28 July of the same year a new refugee convention came into operation.

2

CONVENTIONS AND CATEGORIES
– NEW REFUGEES AND NEW SYSTEMS

[A refugee is defined as]
'Any person who owing to well founded fear of being persecuted for reasons of race, religion, nationality, membership of a particular social group or political opinion, is outside the country of his nationality and is unable, or owing to such fear, is unwilling to avail himself of the protection of that country; or who, not having a nationality and being outside the country of his former habitual residence, is unable, or owing to such fear, is unwilling to return to it.'

– UN Convention on Refugees.

As the major international institution dealing with refugees, UNHCR's main roles are to protect them, and to encourage governments to accept and take responsibility for refugees. UNHCR is a major intergovernmental body upholding the Mandate and Statute on Refugees and has been financed generously by governments. Its other responsibilities include information dissemination, advising decision-making authorities and, more rarely, taking part in the determination of refugee status. In some countries it provides or finances legal advice for asylum-seekers.

In theory, UNHCR is an independent, humanitarian, non-political organization. However its position is delicate as it is financed by states which might try to exert influence to reflect their specific government policies,[20] and it has on its Executive Committee representatives of countries which are themselves responsible for producing refugees.

The 1951 Geneva Convention

With the failure of the League of Nations system to protect individuals because of its emphasis on national groups, the 1951 UN Convention on the Status of Refugees attempted to provide a universal definition.

11

In terms of the Convention a person cannot claim refugee status on the grounds of membership of a particular national group as had been the case up until World War II, but must justify individual persecution on specific grounds. This has been portrayed as a shift to the recognition and protection of individual 'human rights' refugees rather than the collective recognition of 'humanitarian' refugees.[21]

The 1951 Convention defines a refugee as any person who, as a result of events occurring before 1 January 1951 and owing to a well-founded fear of being persecuted for reasons of race, religion, nationality, membership of a particular social group or political opinion, is outside the country of his or her nationality and is unable or, owing to such fear, is unwilling to return to it. In addition to the limitation on time, the Convention also allowed states to decide whether the events referred to were to relate to events 'occurring in Europe' or 'in Europe or elsewhere'. Most states signing the Convention entered a reservation confining the definition to events in Europe.

With its restrictions of time and geography the Convention was intended to address the problems created by the post-World War II turmoils and the Cold War. The High Commissioner's mandate was originally set for three years and it was thought that the refugee crisis facing Europe could be dealt with in a relatively short time. Unfortunately this has not proved to be the case, and the 1951 Convention has remained the major international instrument in the field of refugee law. The 1967 Bellagio Protocol extended the provisions of the Convention to post-1951 events and non- Europeans with the exception of the few signatory states which specified that they maintained the geographical limitation.

Interpreting the Convention and evaluating claims

The Convention's definition lends itself to a variety of interpretations. Its central clause incorporates objective and subjective criteria: not only persecution, but fear of persecution. 'Persecution' is difficult enough to define precisely, but 'fear', even if it has to be 'well-founded', is far more elusive. Although UNHCR has produced a detailed *Handbook on Procedures and Criteria for Determining Refugee Status*,[22] interpretation of the criteria depends on the approach of government officials who make the decisions in line with current state policies.

Such evaluation has changed over time;[23] for instance it seems that many of the Europeans for whom the definition was designed might not have been granted refugee status if the Convention had been applied in the same way as it is today.[24] This reflects both shifting approaches in Western Europe as a result of the changing situation in Eastern Europe and a radical change in attitudes to immigration; the post-war recovery period allowed for the easy absorption of the Hungarians after 1956, the subsequent economic collapse of the 1970s led to restrictions on immigrants into Western Europe, particularly those from the Third World. More recently, Vietnamese asylum-seekers in many cases did not need to justify individual persecution but benefited from a favourable presumption as a group.

The Convention stipulates the obligations of the states to those who are granted refugee status. Most important is the prohibition of *refoulement*: states are prohibited from expelling or returning a refugee to a country where he or she risks persecution. Other clauses detail obligations concerning the delivery of identity documents, employment, education, and welfare. Apart from the non-refoulement clause, these provisions offer states a large measure of flexibility which can range from treatment on a par with nationals to the more limited rights and entitlements accorded to other foreigners. In most European countries refugees enjoy a situation similar to nationals.

One hundred and eight states worldwide are signatory to either the 1951 Convention or the 1967 Protocol, or both.[25] In principle, states which grant the status of refugee are not bound to grant territorial asylum, but in practice European states have done so. All 27 states of the Council of Europe[26] have signed the 1951 Convention, and only Turkey and Hungary have limited Convention status to Europeans.

Of the Eastern European states, only Yugoslavia (as it existed before mid-1991) had signed the Convention and Protocol. More recently, Hungary signed the Convention in 1989, Poland and Romania in 1991. However some of the other states, such as the German Democratic Republic (East Germany), had a clause in their constitutions which granted asylum to people persecuted for 'defending the interests of workers and science', and had accepted refugees who satisfied this criterion.[27] Today the asylum law which applies throughout unified Germany is that of the former Federal Republic of Germany.

Decolonization, underdevelopment and new refugees

The 1967 Protocol reflected historical developments in the Third World resulting from a combination of causes including decolonization, the formation of new states, underdevelopment, class and ethnic conflicts, and superpower rivalries which, together, have been root causes which have led to civil wars, revolutions and dictatorships. Improved and cheaper transport, particularly by air, has made it possible for a growing number of refugees from the Third World to seek asylum in Europe. 'New refugees' they were called as they began to arrive in the 1970s, distinguishing them from their European predecessors.[28]

A strict interpretation of the 1951 Convention does not, however, cover all those who need protection: victims of generalized violence are a major category excluded. In a number of cases such people are protected by UNHCR through a procedure known as 'good offices'. First used in 1957, this procedure was extended by a resolution of the UN General Assembly in 1959 to include all groups of refugees 'who do not come within the competence of the United Nations'.[29] Many of the large groups of refugees in the Third World have benefited from this procedure over the past two decades.

Third World initiatives

With so many refugees originating in the Third World, it is from there that new advances have been made in the legal provisions for refugees. In 1969 the Organization of African Unity (OAU) Convention was adopted which broadens the definition of refugees to include:[30]

'Every person who, owing to external aggression, occupation, foreign domination or events seriously disturbing public order in either part or the whole of his country of origin or nationality, is compelled to leave his place of habitual residence in order to seek refuge in another place outside his country of origin or nationality.'

Most refugees qualifying under this definition have been resettled in countries neighbouring their homeland, particularly in Africa, but increasing numbers have been arriving in Europe in the 1980s. The Cartagena Declaration of 1984[31] which was adopted by the Organization of American States (OAS) in 1985 also contains a broader definition, including:

'Persons who have fled their country because their lives, safety or freedom have been threatened by generalized violence, foreign aggression, internal conflicts, massive violation of human rights or other circumstances which have seriously disturbed the public order.'

Other regional international conventions on asylum concern the American continent but they do not add to the definitions presented above: the 1928 Havana Convention on Asylum; the 1933 Montevideo

Convention on Political Asylum; and the 1954 Caracas Conventions
on Territorial Asylum and Diplomatic Asylum.

Such discrepancies inevitably create some incoherence in the international body of laws. More concretely, they may mean that a genuine
refugee with full status in one part of the world would be considered
ineligible, 'false', elsewhere.

Other categories

Two other categories, not explicitly included in the 1951 Convention,
have been given specific consideration: women and conscientious
objectors to military service. The Executive Committee of the UNHCR
programme indicated in 1985 that states were free to grant refugee status to women on the grounds that they were persecuted as a 'particular
social group' within the terms of the 1951 Convention.

One European country, Sweden, has allowed deserters and war
resisters to seek protection. However, this may change as a result of
proposals introduced by the Swedish government in 1991. The UN
Commission on Human Rights recognized conscientious objection as a
valid expression of human rights which has made it possible in some
cases (USA, Canada) to establish a claim for asylum based on military
desertion.

Other international and European instruments exist which enable
states to offer protection: for example, the 1984 UN Anti-Torture
Convention which has been signed by France, and the 1950 Council of
Europe Convention for the Protection of Human Rights and
Fundamental Freedoms. It has also been argued[32] that the determination of refugee status ought to be based on the violations of the standards of the UN Universal Declaration of Human Rights which stipulates that:

*'Everyone has the right to seek and enjoy in other countries asylum
from persecution.'*

An emerging ethic of human rights

No absolute definition or international law on refugees exists or is possible. Taken together, the conventions and resolutions represent an
internationally accepted ethic of human rights which has emerged in
response to changing circumstances.[33] But the right to asylum is limited even under these conventions. Refugees are guaranteed the right to

'seek' asylum but not to obtain it: it is the sole prerogative of the recipient state to recognize refugees and grant them asylum on its territory.[34]

3

THE NEW REFUGEE:
USING THE CONVENTIONS IN EUROPE

[Governments should]
'act in a particularly liberal and humanitarian spirit in relation to persons who seek asylum on their territory.'

– Resolution 16 (1967) on Asylum to Persons in
Danger of Persecution, Council of Europe.

The scope for interpretation offered by the 1951 Convention has resulted in widely different applications in Europe. Several legal and social categories of 'refugees' have emerged which vary from country to country and whose rights also vary.

Convention refugees are granted refugee status under the 1951 Geneva Convention. They are divided into two groups. Firstly, there are 'quota' refugees who are taken in as a group and under a programme, eg. the Vietnamese. Secondly, there are 'spontaneous' refugees who arrive in Europe of their own accord and make an application for asylum according to a national procedure.

People applying for refugee status are known as *asylum-seekers* while they are awaiting a decision.

Because **Italy** ratified the Refugee Convention and Protocol with a geographical limitation excluding non-Europeans, it was the only European country with *Mandate refugees* recognized under the UNHCR mandate. New legislation in 1990 removed the limitation and mandate refugees were 'converted' into Convention refugees. In other Western European countries there is generally no distinction between Convention and Mandate refugees.

If asylum-seekers are not recognized they are not necessarily expelled. So-called *humanitarian* status refugees are allowed to stay in the country for humanitarian reasons under another status than that of the Convention: 'status B or C' in **Scandinavian** countries; asilo in **Spain**; 'exceptional leave to remain' in the **UK**; assimilé à réfugié in

Belgium; temporary residence permit in **Germany**.[35]

The variety in status in different countries arises from states' ad hoc legal responses to changes in the nature of refugee movements, and an unwillingness on the part of European states to recognize many asylum-seekers under the Convention. The rights enjoyed under such status are generally much more limited than those of Convention refugees; this has caused a debate on their legitimacy.

Many non-governmental organizations (NGOs) argue that humanitarian status is being used as a means of enabling refugees to be settled without the rights and in worse conditions than if they were granted refugee status. In the **UK**, for example, refugees with exceptional leave to remain are not allowed to be joined by their families for four years, while those with Convention status have an immediate right of family reunion.

De facto refugees comprise, in addition to humanitarian refugees, several groups of people who are not recognized refugees but are in a refugee-like situation,[36] and may be hidden in other categories of aliens such as foreign students, migrant workers and visitors.[37] Such people are unable to return to their country of origin but are reluctant to claim refugee status because, for example, they fear reprisals against their families. Asylum-seekers whose applications have been rejected but who have not been deported may also fall into this group which is likely to experience the most severe conditions of settlement.

In a report on de facto refugees, the Council of Europe has expressed its concern about their situation.[38] While acknowledging that such people fall outside the scope of the 1951 Convention, there were valid reasons for their being unable to return. These would include a reasonable belief that they would be unable to exercise their human rights, be discriminated against or be compelled to act in a manner incompatible with their conscience. In addition, war or serious public disorder are advanced as valid reasons for refusal to return.

UNHCR has denounced 'legalistic and static' approaches. People should be given temporary asylum and humane treatment if they have valid reasons for not wanting to return home, even if they do not qualify in terms of the Convention.[39]

'Refugees in orbit' refers to a phenomenon whereby refugees have been sent from country to country with none willing to accept responsibility to examine their request for asylum. A recent convention signed by members of the European Community (EC) may help to overcome this problem.

Who is a refugee? The search for common characteristics

Given the variety of definitions and legal categories, what character-
izes refugees and differentiates them from other migrants? One essential feature is that refugees are involuntary migrants. Several studies
have emphasized this one essential feature pertaining to refugee movements: they did not want to leave.

> *'With a different goal and with motivations at variance with those
> affecting voluntary migrants, the refugee moves from his homeland to
> the country of his settlement against his will. He is a distinct social
> type... It is the reluctance to uproot oneself, and the absence of positive
> original motivations to settle elsewhere, which characterizes all refugee
> decisions and distinguishes the refugee from the voluntary migrants.'*[40]

Kunz argues that this applies whether people are 'anticipatory'
refugees, who foresee the crisis, or 'emergency' refugees, who are victims of it. Zolberg develops a more detailed analysis from a study of
refugee movements worldwide, and identifies three main types: dis-
senters, target groups and bystanders. They share one characteristic
that merges the three categories into a coherent set and distinguishes
them from others: violence.[41] Violence encompasses a range of situations including indirectly inflicted violence, 'by way of imposed conditions that make normal life impossible'. Refugees could be placed on a
spectrum according to the characteristics and acuteness of their situation. Hathaway argues that disenfranchisement from one's home society in a way deemed fundamental, is an element common to all
refugee situations.[42]

The involuntary character of the refugees' departure is not always
easy to identify. For instance, loss of one's livelihood can result from
economic causes like a recession, but particular groups or individuals
may suffer especially because they are deprived of land, employment
or education as a result of political persecution. Natural disasters can
also have discriminatory political consequences.

New realities and the need for new definitions

The realities of the modern refugee phenomenon might justify a re-
evaluation of issues and definitions. Legal definitions and international conventions have evolved to include and exclude varying groups
and individuals on different criteria according to the character of a
particular period.[43]

The 1951 Convention definition with its provisions for recognition on the basis of individual persecution was a response to the horrors of the Holocaust and the realignment of Europe in the aftermath of World War II. But the new Convention did not change the status of refugees recognized under previous agreements, with the result that there were several categories of refugee, each with different official status, in the 1950s. For two decades the 1951 Convention, complemented by the 1967 Protocol, seemed to satisfy the needs of refugees. The definition was interpreted liberally, and immigration policies were relaxed.

But from the early 1970s the strict immigration policies of most European states have added new elements to the question of asylum. Governments and parts of the media have tended to portray asylum-seekers as immigrants in disguise. They fail to note that many immigrants of the 1960s and 1970s were refugees 'in disguise'. Liberal immigration policies allowed them in without their having to claim refugee status, an easier route taken by, for example, many Kurdish and Turkish refugees going to West Germany.

Further complications arise in situations where the same circumstances give rise to both refugees and economic immigrants. Economic depression does indeed cause economic migration, but it can also create unrest resulting in repression and refugee movements.

Although it is not always easy to make clear distinctions between refugees and immigrants, it is essential to do so, as their situation is covered by different national and international legislation and conventions. Closing the borders to non-European immigrants while increasing the pace of European integration has led to stricter and more limited interpretation of the 1951 Convention, precisely at a time when refugee needs have become greater.

It is possible to argue that the 1951 definition meets the needs of refugees who can substantiate a claim of individual persecution. But, as we have seen, other categories of genuine refugees exist who are not covered. Varying categories of refugees were recognized in the past. Moreover, outside Europe there are more recent conventions with wider scope.

A major debate centres on the issue of whether the 1951 Convention is adequate, or whether it should be revised or complemented by European agreements incorporating criteria to be found in the UN Universal Declaration of Human Rights, the UN Convention Against Torture, the OAU Convention and the Council of Europe Recommendations and Resolutions.

Opponents of any change, particularly among NGOs, argue that the

1951 Geneva definition can accommodate all refugees if it is liberally interpreted. In addition, they fear that, given present trends, European states would take advantage of any opportunity to introduce measures which would be even more restrictive.

As will be argued later, there are good grounds for these fears; and they have become more pressing because of the potential eruption of refugee movements from within Europe itself. Eastern Europeans fleeing from the violence surrounding the disintegration of the old order cannot always substantiate claims to individual persecution but may fall within other categories. Can they be accommodated, and how will this be reconciled with present policies which have been constructed to keep refugees out? Before looking at these issues, however the number and origins of refugees in Europe should be examined.

4

ARRIVALS AND RECOGNITION: REFUGEE NUMBERS

'there are three kinds of lies – lies, damned lies and statistics...'

– Mark Twain

Comprehensive and reliable statistics on refugees in Europe are difficult to assemble. Some of the issues concerning the compilation of refugee statistics are methodological; others are influenced by the ways in which decisions are made and the overall view compiling states wish to give.

Not only do different countries have different categories under which refugees are recognized, but they keep records in different ways and at varying levels of detail. Some aggregate asylum-seekers and refugees, others keep separate records; sometimes only the head of a family which is recognized as refugee is counted, sometimes every family member. People can even be counted twice: once when they apply for asylum, and again when they are granted refugee status.[44] In many countries figures are not broken down, making it difficult to identify the numbers from different national groups settled in particular countries. It has been argued that the number of refugees in Western Europe is grossly exaggerated.[45]

Despite these limitations, and with a caveat that the figures are not completely reliable, it is possible to piece together figures which give a broad indication of the situation since 1975. From these figures a number of trends can be identified.

A growing need for protection

The most obvious trend is a great rise in the number of people seeking asylum in Europe.[46] In 1972 there were some 13,000; by 1988 there were 232,000. There were particularly sharp rises in 1979 up to 77,600, and the following year when the number more than doubled to 158,500.[47]

23

Figure 1 **Asylum-seekers in Europe 1984-88**

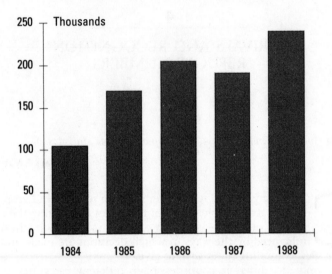

Figure 2 **Asylum-seekers in selected Western European countries: Region of origin**

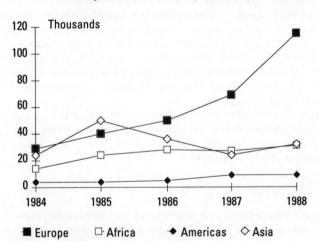

Europe = Austria, Belgium, Denmark, France, Federal Republic of Germany, Netherlands, Norway, Sweden, Switzerland, United Kingdom

Figure 1 illustrates the growth in the period between 1984 and 1988. **Figure 2** breaks down the numbers from the various regions of origin and shows how these have fluctuated over the years. **Figure 3** contrasts the number of asylum-seekers in 1985 and 1990 in the main European countries and gives an estimate for 1991. Between 1989 and 1990, seven northern European countries have experienced increases in the numbers of asylum-seekers (**Belgium, Denmark, Finland, Germany, Netherlands,** Switzerland, UK), the three exceptions being **France, Norway** and **Sweden**, as illustrated by **Table 1**. In recent years there has also been an increase in the number of asylum-seekers in southern Europe (**Greece, Italy, Spain** and pre-1991 **Yugoslavia**), rising from 16,000 in 1986 to 23,000 in 1987.[48]

While there have undoubtedly been large increases over the past decade, the numbers appear less dramatic when viewed in the global context. There are less than a million refugees in Western Europe – an insignificant number compared to the 20 million immigrants.[49] Refugees settled in Europe also comprise less than 10% of the world refugee population of 16 million, most of whom are to be found in the poorer regions of the Third World.[50] Most refugees are 'regionalized', moving into neighbouring countries: in Asia, 6,563,500; in Africa 3,974,400; and in the Americas 1,685,000. Finally refugees comprise a tiny proportion, only 0.17% of the population of Western Europe.[51] These trends are summarized in **Figure 4**.

The capacity of countries to assist and absorb refugees also needs to be considered in relation to wealth and population density. **Figure 4** compares the situation in some European countries with some of the major refugee recipient nations in the Third World.

The trend towards increased numbers has not been consistent and has been affected by the response of European governments, which is discussed later in this book. Despite their already relatively poor record, restrictive measures have been introduced in most European states in an attempt to lessen the number of asylum-seekers. This appeared to be effective, with numbers dropping to 188,750 in 1987 compared to 205,600 the previous year. However, numbers increased again to 236,500 in 1988.

On the whole, asylum-seekers are unevenly distributed. **Figure 5** illustrates the countries in which the 789,500 applications for asylum were made in 1984 and 1988. **West Germany** accounted for nearly half, followed by **France** and **Sweden**.

The main groups applying for asylum also vary between countries. Overall the major countries of origin of asylum-seekers between 1984 and 1987 are illustrated in **Table 2**.

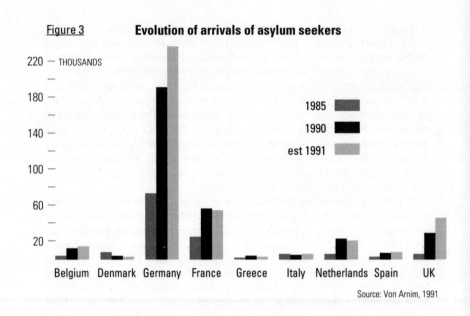

Figure 3   **Evolution of arrivals of asylum seekers**

1985
1990
est 1991

Belgium   Denmark   Germany   France   Greece   Italy   Netherlands   Spain   UK

Source: Von Arnim, 1991

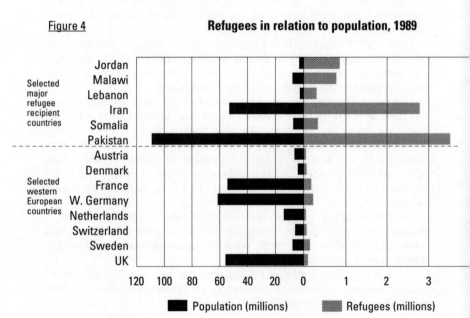

Figure 4   **Refugees in relation to population, 1989**

Selected major refugee recipient countries: Jordan, Malawi, Lebanon, Iran, Somalia, Pakistan

Selected western European countries: Austria, Denmark, France, W. Germany, Netherlands, Switzerland, Sweden, UK

120 100 80 60 40 20 0   1   2   3

Population (millions)   Refugees (millions)

Table 1

Applicants for asylum in some West European countries, 1989-90

Country	1989	1990
Belgium	8,112	12,964
Denmark	4,588	5,292
Finland	179	2,725
France	61,372	56,053
Germany	121,318	193,063
Netherlands	13,898	21,208
Norway	4,400	3,962
Sweden	30,335	29,420
Switzerland	24,425	35,836
UK	11,465	22,000

Source: ECRE, March 1991 and Refugee Council, 1992

Table 2

Major countries of origin of asylum seekers

Country	1984	1987
Poland		39,105
Turkey		34,380
Yugoslavia	24,029	
Iran	16,926	
Sri Lanka	7,675	
Lebanon		6,480
Chile	6,311	
Ghana		5,029

Figure 5

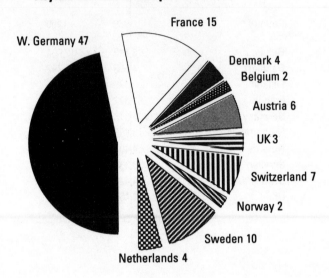

Asylum-seekers in Europe 1984-88 (%)

W. Germany 47 France 15 Denmark 4 Belgium 2 Austria 6 UK 3 Switzerland 7 Norway 2 Sweden 10 Netherlands 4

In **Sweden** and **Norway**, the two main groups of asylum-seekers, far ahead of the others, were from Chile and Iran; in **France** from Turkey and Sri Lanka; in the **UK** from Turkey and Iran; and in **Austria** from Poland.

In 1990, the nationality of most asylum-seekers continued to differ according to the country of reception: sub-Saharan Africans in **Belgium** and **France**, stateless Palestinians in **Denmark**, Somalis in **Finland**, various Europeans, including Turks in **Germany**, Sri Lankans in the **Netherlands**, Yugoslavs (ie. from pre-1991 Yugoslavia) in **Norway**, Lebanese in **Sweden** and Turks in **Switzerland**.[52]

There is also a great discrepancy where actual numbers are concerned; while **Germany** received 81,760 asylum-seekers from the main countries of origin (already indicated) in 1988, the UK received 566 (the lowest figure for the northern European countries); while **Sweden** received 3384 Chileans, **Austria** received only 14 and the UK five;

Table 3

Applications for asylum in the UK, 1989-91

	1989	1990	1991
EUROPE AND AMERICAS	2,655	1,865	3,875
Of which:			
Turkey	2,360	1,100	2,110
AFRICA	5,060	9,430	27,490
Of which:			
Ethiopia	560	1,840	1,685
Ghana	325	790	2,405
Somalia	1,845	1,850	1,995
Sudan	110	220	1,150
Togo/Ivory Coast	20	85	1,910
Uganda	1,240	1,895	1,440
Zaire	490	1,490	7,010
MIDDLE EAST	780	2,340	2,540
ASIA	2,875	6,520	10,405
Of which:			
India	630	1,415	2,045
Pakistan	250	1,295	3,195
Sri Lanka	1,785	3,325	3,750
OTHERS	100	1,845	435
Total	11,465	22,000	44,745

NB. Applications do not include dependents and all figures are rounded to the nearest 5.
There are slight discrepancies in measuring figures for 1990 and 1991.

Source: Refugee Council, 1992.

while **France** and **Germany** respectively received 1498 and 3383 asylum-seekers from Sri Lanka, the **UK** had only 74.[53]

It is in the nature of refugee movements that total numbers and patterns change over time. In the **UK** the numbers rose from 11,465 in 1989 to 44,745 in 1991 as illustrated in **Table 3**. Most of the new applicants came from areas of Africa undergoing violent conflict.

Numbers of asylum-seekers from **Eastern Europe** have also increased, rising from 29,065 in 1984 to 115,662 in 1988 (see **Figure 2**). By the 1990s the figures had increased even more dramatically.

5

RECOGNIZING REFUGEES:
DECISIONS ON ASYLUM APPLICATIONS

*The Contracting States shall not impose penalties, on account of their
illegal entry or presence, on refugees who, coming directly from a territory where their life or freedom was threatened in the sense of Article 1,
enter or are present in their territory without authorization, provided
they present themselves without delay to the authorities and show good
cause for their illegal entry or presence.'*

> – Article 31, UN Convention on Refugees.

At the beginning of 1988 there were in Europe an estimated
737,600 refugees recognized under the Convention.[54] This figure is misleading as it includes people who have been natural-
ized and have thus lost their status as refugees. Some of these
may, however, still consider themselves to be refugees and would
return to their countries of origin if circumstances allowed.

Figure 6 shows the pattern of decisions on asylum in the period
1984-8.[55] It illustrates very clearly the decline in the number of asylum-
seekers granted refugee status and the growth in the number of rejections. According to one UNHCR memorandum from 1988, the average
rate of recognition in Europe is 35% and a further 20% are permitted
to stay on humanitarian grounds.[56]

But rates of recognition vary by over 50% depending on the country
concerned: in 1985 **Denmark** recognized 72% of applicants while
France recognized 31% and the **UK**, 17%.[57] **Figure 7** breaks down the
decisions made in four countries: France, Germany, Switzerland and
the UK. They reflect the general trend towards an increase in the number of refusals and greater use of humanitarian status rather than full
recognition. In 1990 there was a further decrease in rates of recognition to 15% in **France**, 3.2% in **Norway**, 3.5% in **Switzerland** and
5.3% in **Germany**.[58]

Figure 6

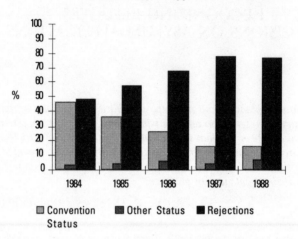

Decisions on asylum applications 1984-88

☐ Convention Status   ■ Other Status   ■ Rejections

New attempts to harmonize European procedures

Refugees present a complex issue, bringing into play a variety of potentially conflicting policies. Granting asylum is a human rights and humanitarian issue. But there are also security considerations and social and economic consequences, with the result that governments make political decisions about refugees which may not always accord with humanitarian principles.

All European states use the 1951 Convention as the basis for their decisions. But it is, ultimately, the individual state which decides whether or not to grant asylum and refugee status; and decisions cannot be detached from the political considerations that a particular government holds paramount. Rates of recognition of refugees vary with regard to a combination of the country of reception,[59] the country of origin of the refugees, and the policies of the government currently in power. Discrepancies can prove astonishingly vast as demonstrated by the case of Tamil asylum-seekers, **France** granting 50% of them refugee status whereas the **Netherlands** only recognized 3%.[60]

The nature of the government can fundamentally alter policies: eg. in the UK the then Conservative government did not accept Chilean refugees in the aftermath of the 1973 coup; between 1974 and 1979 the succeeding Labour government admitted 3000 in an organized programme, which in turn was terminated six months after the re-election of the Conservatives in 1979.

From a foreign policy viewpoint, the decision to accept refugees will be influenced by the relationship with other states, including international alliances, 'camps', military pacts and trade agreements. Western countries often like to pose as 'terres d' asile' in order to demonstrate the 'superiority' of Western democracy compared to some military dictatorships in the Third World or to communist regimes.

A particular decision may be dictated by a specific set of international conditions and also by publicity considerations; eg. the UK accepted 10,000 Vietnamese refugees from Hong Kong in 1979, but started forcible repatriation to Vietnam from Hong Kong ten years later, to suspend the operation only in the wake of an international outcry.

Foreign policy considerations also affect decisions on individual cases. Information on the country of origin of applicants is partly provided by embassies whose main brief is to ensure good relations with the countries concerned, not to monitor their human rights records.

Domestic policies and politics bring other forces to bear; in the early 1990s the main concerns are those related to immigration and state security. Refugees are central in many debates about immigration, but they are rarely distinguished from immigrants. Decisions are more likely to be dictated by labour requirements and the need for specific skills than by refugees' needs for protection. Demographic considerations may also be taken into account as in France during the inter-war period.

States fear that the admission of a particular group of refugees may set a precedent, thus creating a 'pull effect'[61] attracting even greater numbers. The country of origin and the ethnic or racial background of refugees also play a part as European countries are more hesitant to accept non-European refugees.

Differences of opinion also exist between different departments of national government. For instance, in most European states the foreign office has the reputation of being more flexible and open than the home office or interior ministry on the question of refugees. Refugee agencies know this and make use of such discrepancies, playing on inconsistencies and contradictions to promote their point of view.

Political manoeuvring of this kind makes decisions on the basis of human rights principles difficult, and multiplies the possibility of vari-

<u>Figure 7</u>

Asylum decisions

France

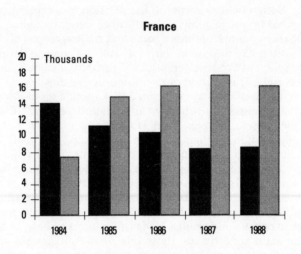

Switzerland

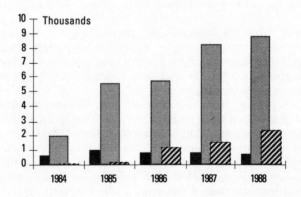

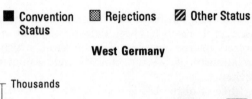

West Germany

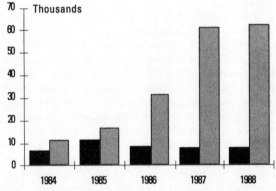

United Kingdom

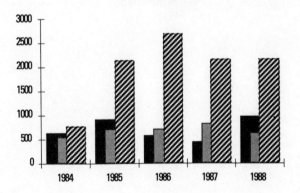

ations in the interpretation of the Convention. Different national traditions complicate the matter still further.

Defending the right to asylum

The right to asylum has come under threat from the actions of states in the past decade. But it has been defended by concerned individuals and organizations and, in particular, by those which are concerned with the relationship between democratic rights, human rights and the right of asylum.

Former Director of the UN Human Rights Centre Theo Van Boven[62] suggests that the degree of solidarity of a society can be measured by its attitude towards the vulnerable and marginalized, and it is the NGOs that support their interests. Gérard Soulier argues that the right of asylum is *'preuve et garant du droit démocratique'* ('proof and guarantee of democratic right'), counterposing it to the interest of states because, expressed crudely in the words of the former French Interior Minister Charles Pasqua *'la démocratie s'arrêté aù commence la raison d'Etat'* ('democracy stops where the reason of state starts').[63]

Indeed, large sectors of society have supported asylum-seekers; the sanctuary movement (where asylum-seekers are sheltered and helped to remain in the host country) testifies to this as well as the campaigns launched in several European countries to defend the right of asylum. Trade unions, Churches, women's organizations and others have all made a contribution. However, society itself is not homogeneous and sections of it have sometimes turned against refugees – as in the Swiss referendum on refugees and in the referendum in the town of Sjobo in Sweden, described in the following chapter.

6

RESTRICTIONS:
A COMMON TREND

'Everyone has the right to seek and enjoy in other countries asylum from persecution.'

– Article 14, UN Universal Declaration of Human Rights.

Governments in Western Europe have become concerned with the increase and unpredictability of asylum-seekers' arrivals in Europe. This has contributed to a chain reaction of similar restrictive measures throughout Western Europe.

Economic recession and unemployment have often been put forward to account for this trend, but alone, they do not seem to provide sufficient explanation: **Norway** became one of the strictest countries for asylum-seekers (certainly by far the strictest of the Nordic states) at a time when there was practically no unemployment.

Another argument advanced is that public opinion has put pressure on governments to tighten controls. This remains debatable for it is individual members of the public or groups who have defended the right of asylum. It is true, however, that local populations have at times demonstrated hostility towards refugees. For example, a 1990 referendum amongst the 15,000 residents of Sjobo in **Sweden** decided against the acceptance of 15 Iranian refugees, although ironically this led to widespread national condemnation of their stance, and public support for refugees.[64]

Moreover, it has become clear that in Western Europe 'public opinion' itself is strongly influenced by government decisions and, overall, by the media. Large headlines on the 'hordes of bogus refugees' are likely to trigger an adverse reaction, while compassionate images of the plight of boat people have been shown to gain public sympathy. Whatever the reasons, two trends have emerged. Firstly, governments have introduced measures to curb the number of asylum-seekers; secondly, after an initial decrease, the numbers have continued to rise.

Restrictive measures: general immigration laws

Refugees have been affected by general immigration laws implemented in the late 1980s in several European countries. In **Belgium** the 18 July 1991 law modified a 1980 law, relating to access to the territory, residence, settlement and extradition of foreigners, with particular regard to refugees.[65] **Denmark**, which had one of the most liberal asylum policies, adopted new legislation in 1983. A 1986 amendment to the Aliens Act introduced the concept of 'safe countries' to which asylum-seekers could be returned – a concept which has been severely questioned by NGOs – and the 1988 Aliens Act considerably increased restrictions.[66] In **Germany** a new Aliens Law was passed on 1 January 1991. **Finland**'s Aliens Act was passed on 15 February 1991 and, against the trend, seems to bring in some improvements for asylum-seekers.[67] In France, in 1986, tighter legal proposals for asylum-seekers were foiled after the intervention of NGOs.[68]

The Netherlands government introduced a Bill before Parliament containing a completely new aliens law relating to refugees which, according to NGOs, has been influenced by the Schengen proposals[69] (examined in Chapter 14). A very restrictive new Aliens Act came into force in **Norway** in January 1990. In the **UK** the 1988 Immigration Act limits the use of 'compassionate circumstances' by asylum-seekers threatened with deportation,[70] and **Sweden** revised its Aliens Act in 1989. A new asylum law was approved by a **Swiss** plebiscite in April 1987 and the following year an amendment to the Aliens Act created an accelerated procedure for irregular arrivals which was primarily directed at Turks.[71] The proposed British Asylum Bill, examined below, was postponed in the light of the general election in April 1992 but the re-elected Conservative government has declared its intention to proceed with a similar measure.

Restrictive measures: visas and deportations

In addition to general immigration legislation a variety of measures have been adopted in Europe with the aim of reducing the numbers of asylum-seekers.

Most states have imposed visas on nationals of refugee-producing countries. On 1 January 1989, **Sweden** imposed visas on Chileans who constituted its second largest group of asylum-seekers. **Denmark** imposed visas on Romanians in January 1989 after 230 Romanians arrived from Hungary in the last months of 1988.[72] **Belgium** introduced compulsory visas for entrants from the principal countries of origin of its asylum-seekers in 1983 and this was extended to other countries in 1986.[73]

The **UK** imposed visas on Sri Lankans in 1985 after the persecution of Tamils had become widespread, a requirement later extended to nationals of India, Bangladesh, Ghana, Nigeria and Pakistan. From June 1989 visas were required from nationals of Turkey after more than 4000 Turkish Kurds had filed applications for asylum on arrival. In July 1988, **Norway** imposed visa requirements on Chilean nationals who made up the largest group of new asylum-seekers (46%).

France was strictest – imposing visa requirements on all non-EC citizens, apart from Swiss nationals. More recently, transit visas have been introduced for the same reason. In July 1991, France requested transit visas from nationals of 11 countries: Albania, Angola, Bangladesh, Ethiopia, Ghana, Haiti, Nigeria, Pakistan, Somalia, Sri Lanka and Zaire. These are countries producing substantial numbers of asylum-seekers.

In some cases agreements have been struck between several countries to prevent the arrival of asylum-seekers. In the most important arrangement of this kind, made in 1985, people from the Near East, Middle East and Southeast Asia could receive a transit visa from the **German Democratic Republic** only if they had a valid entry visa for Denmark or Sweden.[74] In 1987 an agreement between East and West Germany closed the 'Berlin gap' through which asylum-seekers entered Western Europe.

Visa requirements have been strengthened by the legislation providing for fines on airlines or other transporters. Some states felt that the Chicago Convention on International Civil Aviation, which makes airline companies responsible for the cost of flying back passengers without valid papers, was insufficient. **Denmark** (October 1988 amendment of the Aliens Act), **Germany** (since 1986) and the **UK** (May 1987 Carriers Liability Act) imposed heavy fines on companies carrying undocumented passengers. In Germany repeated offences may lead to a company losing its licence to fly certain routes.

While governments may argue that these measures are not aimed at asylum-seekers but are designed to control immigration, it remains evident that asylum-seekers are most seriously affected as it is more difficult for many of them to obtain valid passports and visas.[75]

In some cases visitors requesting entry into a country have to show a return ticket and sufficient money to cover their stay; these were requirements imposed by **Spain** in 1989 because it found it difficult to impose visas on Latin American countries with which it maintains special relations. It was alleged that, at one stage, 30,000 Latin Americans were refused entry to Spain until a protest was raised by NGOs and Latin American governments.

On other occasions, police have examined passports on aeroplanes, prevented potential asylum-seekers from leaving the plane, or stopped them from leaving the international area of the airport. This prevents people from making an application for asylum, a process which can only be initiated on national territory. Kurds returned to Turkey in this manner have taken the **UK** government to court for a breach of the 1951 Convention.[76]

If asylum-seekers manage to reach Europe despite these hurdles, they may still be sent back without being given a chance to make a proper application. A number of refugees are secretly refouled; but a few dramatic cases have been uncovered. A Lebanese asylum-seeker, forcibly returned from **Denmark** in June 1988, was kidnapped on arrival in Beirut and disappeared.[77] In 1989 five Tamils, whose cases had gone on appeal to the House of Lords, were deported from the **UK**. Three were detained and tortured in Sri Lanka and the other two went into hiding.[78] ECRE quotes 50 forcible returns from the UK in the first half of 1988,[79] and several Turks were sent back home from Germany. In the UK, where Members of Parliament have the right to intervene to stop summary deportation, limitations were imposed in 1989.[80]

Sometimes asylum-seekers are returned to so-called countries of first asylum where they face being sent back to the country from which they fled: four Iranians were sent to Turkey after being returned to **West Germany** by **Denmark**; and 15 Tamils were sent to India where they faced immediate imprisonment after being returned by Denmark via Finland and Poland. These are only a few of the numerous instances of this kind.[81]

The 'country of first asylum' rule has contributed to increases in the number of deportations: if an asylum-seeker has passed through a country where he is deemed to have been able to find protection, his application may not be accepted when he arrives in Europe. **Austria, Belgium, Denmark, Switzerland** and **Sweden** have integrated the principle of 'country of first asylum' with their legislation on asylum, although they do not implement it in the same manner. In the **Netherlands** and **Belgium**, to be eligible to apply for asylum the asylum-seeker must not have sojourned more than three months in a first asylum country, and in **Germany**, staying more than three months in another country may provide a reason for rejection at the German border. The principle of country of first asylum is interpreted very strictly in **Norway** and **Denmark**; in the latter, according to amendments to the Act of October 1986, one hour in transit is sufficient for the rule of first asylum country to be applied, which entails the return of the asylum-seeker to the country of transit.

Refugees recognized under the 1951 Convention have also been expelled. In one of the most extreme cases, in **France**, one Turkish and 10 Iranian refugees, together with four asylum-seekers and two foreign residents, were removed to Gabon in December 1987. After a massive public outcry from within France and abroad they were allowed to return.[82]

States have even extradited refugees or asylum-seekers although this appears to contravene the non-refoulement clause of the Geneva Convention. Between 19 July 1986 and 11 March 1987 France extradited 50 Spanish Basques to Spain where they were apprehended by the police and kept in custody for questioning. Some had testified to Amnesty International that they had been tortured.[83] As the result of a ruling by the *Conseil d'Etat* in April 1988 that a statutory refugee cannot be extradited to his/her country of origin, such actions are no longer possible.[84]

When refugees do finally gain entry into a European country, they may find that making an application for asylum is far from easy. In **Switzerland**, for example, there are only four border points at which an application can be made. In many countries a lack of interpreters can delay an application for so long that the legal deadlines have expired before it can be presented.[85]

Restrictive measures: 'deterrence'

A number of so-called 'deterrence measures' have been introduced to discourage asylum-seekers from coming to particular countries.

One set of measures limits asylum-seekers' freedom of movement, among them enforced detention. Although most European countries have legal provisions for detention these have not been extensively used except in **Finland**, **Denmark** and the **UK**. In **Finland** 80% of asylum-seekers appear to have been detained, and in the first half of 1986, 291 people were detained in **Denmark**, of whom 37 were kept in detention for more than two months.[86]

But the position is worst in the **UK** where, as a group, asylum-seekers 'spend longer in prison than anyone else held under Immigration Act powers'.[87] They are detained in Harmondsworth Detention Centre (near Heathrow airport) which can hold 96 persons, or in ordinary prisons when the latter is full. Asylum-seekers were also kept for a time on a car-ferry off Harwich, the *Earl William*, which almost capsized when the hurricane of October 1987 broke the boat's moorings and swept it on to the high seas; its inmates were transferred on to land after this incident.

The use of detention is growing. It is now **Sweden** that keeps asylum-seekers in detention in ships offshore in Malmö and Göteborg, where some cases have involved the division of families and the detention of children. This has raised humanitarian and legal concerns,[88] which have been dealt with in the 1989 Swedish Aliens Act. In **Switzerland** and **Sweden** detention/reception facilities include tents. In **Norway** there is an increased use of detention during the appeal stage. In **Greece**, asylum-seekers entering the country irregularly are imprisoned.[89] The Dutch Aliens Bill made it possible to detain asylum-seekers entering the **Netherlands** by ship or by air and those who receive a negative decision within four weeks of the registration of their application.[90]

The movements of asylum-seekers may also be limited in other ways. In **Denmark** and **Switzerland** they are offered no choice of residence and are compulsorily housed in reception centres. Social assistance is tied to living in assigned residences in the **Netherlands, Sweden,** and **Belgium.**[91] In **Germany**, the federal government admits that a number of measures are designed to reduce the country's 'attractiveness', including a compulsory period in camps, a prohibition on employment, and restricted rights to move and to welfare benefits.[92] Since 1988 asylum-seekers in **France** have been excluded from social housing.

The limitation of their rights can be considered as a clear deterrent for asylum-seekers. While they were previously allowed to work one month after submitting their application in **France** and after six months in the **UK**, asylum-seekers were not permitted to work for the duration of the asylum procedure (which may take several years) in **Denmark, Italy, Spain, Germany** and the **Netherlands.**[93] However, as asylum-seekers acquired the right to work in **Germany** in 1991, they lost it in **France**, where it appeared that policy-makers were intent on pleasing some sections of the electorate who saw asylum-seekers as competitors for employment.

'De facto' or 'humanitarian status' refugees have even fewer rights. In **Germany** the de facto/humanitarian status does not include family reunification provisions. In the **UK** changes have been introduced regarding the exceptional leave to remain which can be deemed to constitute deterrence: refugees will have to wait four years before they can be joined by their spouses or children; and they will have to live in the **UK** for seven years instead of four before they can apply for permanent residence. In **Norway** the vast majority of refugees, who are granted residence on humanitarian grounds, will have to prove that they can support their families before they are allowed into the country.[94]

Restrictive measures: interpreting the 1951 Convention

Stricter interpretation of international obligations can be used as a means to keep down the number of refugees recognized under the 1951 Convention. In most European countries the rate of acceptance of refugees has decreased considerably in the last ten years. This may have occurred either because a smaller number of applicants were genuine or because state practices have become more severe.

Discrepancies in interpretation were studied in detail in the ECRE European lawyers workshop on the implementation of Article 1a of the Geneva Convention.[95] One lawyer argued[96] that there was excessive emphasis laid on the objective criteria, and concluded that the spirit of the Geneva Convention was no longer respected.

According to the Convention the applicant has to demonstrate 'well-founded fear of persecution', and it appears that officers interviewing asylum-seekers increasingly ask them for tangible proof of persecution. Yet such proof is not always considered sufficient as evidence, as illustrated in the case of a Chilean who was not accepted in spite of evidence from psychiatrists that he had been tortured.[97]

In **Germany** the so-called 'objectivity doctrine' prevails, which holds that the determining factor is whether the perpetrator of persecution was politically motivated or not. This may mean, for example, that asylum will only be granted when torture is politically motivated.[98]

Whereas the rate of Convention refugee recognition has diminished, the rate of recognition of humanitarian status refugees has increased considerably. Here again it may be either that such refugees have come to Europe in greater numbers or that people really entitled to Convention status have been transferred into the other inferior categories. There is some evidence for the latter argument: when the **Netherlands** abolished B status the number of refugees recognized under the Convention increased.[99]

Restrictive measures: different national approaches

Legislation and national procedures display significant variance, largely because the 1951 Geneva Convention does not contain procedures for determining refugee status.

In some countries, such as the **UK**, **Ireland** and **Denmark**, refugees come under immigration laws and their appended rules; in others, such as **France**, the 1951 Convention has been incorporated into national law and a specific body deals with asylum-seekers and refugees (*Office Français pour les Réfugiés et Apatrides*, OFPRA). **Belgium** has followed this model in its new structures. In **Germany** the right to asylum is written into the constitution as it is in **France** and in **Italy**. But in the latter no law makes it effective.

In some countries the border authorities or those responsible for immigrants are authorized to decide whether an application is admissible – as in **Germany, Belgium**, and the **UK** where, in addition, there are no precise criteria to determine admissibility.[100] In **France** and **Germany** asylum-seekers cannot be deported while an appeal is being heard, but they can be – and have been – in the **UK**. The **Netherlands** and **Denmark** use a shortened procedure for 'manifestly unfounded' cases. In most countries, however, the procedure can take a very long time: an average of one year in **Belgium, Spain** and **Italy**, two years in **France**, the **UK** and the **Netherlands**, and up to seven years in **Germany** if one includes appeals.[101]

The concept of 'family' is interpreted in different ways. Under the **Danish** interpretation the family includes the spouse and minor dependants, while in **France** it also includes elderly dependants and the common-law spouse. Possibilities of family reunion will clearly be affected by these interpretations. The concept of persecution of kin will also be affected; and in France, Germany and Denmark this is accepted as a valid reason for granting asylum.[102]

Conscientious objectors have been tolerated in **Germany** and the **UK**.[103] Women have sometimes been granted asylum as 'special groups' within the terms of the 1951 Convention but this applies to a few limited individual cases.[104]

Settlement or resettlement (when the refugees have spent some time in a first country of asylum) varies greatly according to the country of reception. Settlement policies have been more heterogeneous than anything else regarding refugees and settlement is the one area which governments have never mentioned in their European consultation on harmonization.

Specific origins, specific destinations

Some European countries have been faced with particular refugee problems which are not relevant to other European states. **Portugal, Spain** and **Greece** have witnessed the return of their nationals who had been refugees elsewhere. **France** and **Spain** have been involved in both open and secret negotiations on Spanish Basque refugees in France. **Italy** and **Austria** have granted temporary asylum to people who were supposed to be settled in other countries.[105]

These latter countries, as well as **Greece**, are traditionally transit countries but this situation is beginning to change as asylum-seekers find it increasingly difficult to move on.[106] Growing numbers of asylum-seekers are living clandestinely in **Italy** (in Lombardy) after being returned by the Swiss authorities. **France** has also had to deal with the arrival of Surinamese refugees in neighbouring French Guiana – 9000 in 1988.[107]

The **UK** has been closely involved with the position of Vietnamese refugees in Hong Kong, and with the potential exodus which may result when the colony reverts to China in 1997, a situation exacerbated by the crushing of the student protests in China in June 1989. The plight of the Vietnamese refugees provoked an international outcry when the British government forcibly repatriated some 50 asylum-seekers in late 1989. After being suspended, forcible repatriations resumed in a trail of violence towards the end of 1991. Voluntary repatriation for those whose applications have been rejected is continuing.

Germany's attitude to refugees is considerably affected by its commitment to assist and absorb ethnic Germans from other parts of Europe. In addition to the large number of asylum applications received from outside Europe, Germany also absorbed people of German descent from Eastern Europe (*Aussiedler*). Before unification in November 1990, East Germans automatically had a right to live in West Germany, and after unification all became citizens of the Federal German Republic.

Finally, the issue of asylum between EC member states was raised when Alan Tyrrell, MEP, presented a report in the name of the Legal Commission of the European Parliament arguing that the right of asylum had no *raison d'être* between the democracies of the EC. According to this EC nationals should not be able to obtain asylum in other EC states. However, this proposition does not seem to have been acceptable to the Parliament.[108]

45

7

REFUGEE SETTLEMENT IN EUROPE: THE ISSUES

'If I should revert to a theme, it is to the universality of our problems and the universality of the effort that is demanded of us. I have heard the words "burden-sharing" wherever I have travelled. They should never serve as an alibi, for any of us, to do less than we can. Above all, we must resist the tendency to think that there are facile, general solutions...'

– Poul Hartling, former UN High Commissioner for Refugees.

Although governments have not given priority to conditions of settlement, international conventions, refugee agencies and NGOs place considerable emphasis on this area. The 1951 Geneva Convention stipulates the obligations of states which grant refugee status and makes a number of recommendations regarding employment and welfare which include rationing, housing, education, public relief and all aspects of health and social security. The UN Universal Declaration of Human Rights also makes a case for satisfactory conditions of living: Article 25 (1) states that:

'Everyone has the right to a standard of living adequate for the health and well-being of himself and of his family, including food, clothing, housing and medical care and necessary social services, and the right to security in the event of unemployment, sickness, disability, widowhood, old age or other lack of livelihood in circumstances beyond his control.'[109]

The Declaration also includes the right to employment and education.

In Europe, both the European Parliament and the Council of Europe have concerned themselves with refugees and asylum-seekers' conditions of settlement, stressing the importance of this issue.[110]

The question of settlement is a fundamental one from several points of view. Firstly, in terms of the Geneva Convention, states undertake to meet certain minimum standards. People should not only be granted admission, but should be enabled to lead a normal life. In a paradoxical argument, lack of settlement facilities has sometimes been used as a reason for limiting the number of places offered to refugees,[111] making the issue of even greater importance for them. Good conditions of settlement throughout European countries could also contribute to reducing the imbalance in the distribution of refugees and asylum-seekers.

Satisfactory settlement is not only beneficial for refugees but also for the societies in which they settle. Positive policies enable refugees to make a contribution instead of being a potential burden. A dramatic example which illustrates the point is the 15 Nobel Prizes won by refugees who have settled in the UK.[112] There are many more examples of valuable, albeit less spectacular, contributions made by refugees and these will be examined below.

Discussing settlement and developing adequate policies is more easily said than done. There has been little systematic study of the settlement process. Policy-makers rarely seem to have learned from previous experiences in their own country and few appear to have heard of the situation in neighbouring countries.[113] The wheel has to be reinvented for each group of new refugee arrivals. Unfortunately the existence and arrival of refugees are more likely to be consistent than transient features of today's world.

In addition, little is known of the needs of refugees, in view of the dearth of research. In any case the issue is a complex one because the refugee population is not homogenous and multiple factors are likely to influence the process of settlement. Some of the main elements which need to be considered are outlined below.

Factors influencing settlement

Family
The larger proportion of spontaneous refugees are single men but quota refugees often come as a family and single people can eventually be joined by their family when family reunion is permitted. It has been noticed that single refugees sometimes integrate more rapidly than families as they are more likely to find a native partner, but they can also find themselves much more isolated and lack the emotional support which a family most often provides.

The UNHCR has stressed the importance of a generous policy on family reunification as 'the emotional stability of the refugee and his family is an indispensable basis for any successful integration process'.[114] Without doubt, anxieties about the fate of relatives are not conducive to satisfactory settlement. The particular role and structure of the family in specific cultures needs examination.

In many cases, however, families have not been able to stand the strain of exile and contradictions have developed between husband and wife, children and parents.[115] More recently the arrival of unaccompanied minors has brought in a new category of people whose process of settlement is quite specific.

Age and gender
Age and gender have to be taken into account: refugee agency workers single out women, young people and the elderly for their respective specific needs. The elderly may find it more difficult to learn a new language and socialize,[116] as may refugee women, especially if they are housewives. As a consequence they run the risk of finding themselves very isolated, particularly if they come from cultures where they are accustomed to a close-knit and extended family network. Young people may want opportunities for a variety of activities and need special assistance to adapt to a new education system.[117]

Socio-economic background
The level of education and the socio-economic background are equally important. A good level of education can be an advantage as the experience of studying often makes it easier to learn a new language, and literacy in one's own language certainly facilitates literacy in another. However it can also lead to disillusionment since it is difficult for professional refugees to obtain employment in their own field and at the same level, at least initially.[118]

On the other hand, unskilled persons may be more prepared to begin with any job they find and thereafter improve their situation. Yet their plight is aggravated by the fact that they are at a disadvantage when compared to other workers because they do not speak the language. On the whole, the key question will be the transferability of employment skills and experience.

History of migration
The history of the individual or family will influence the process of settlement. People who have stayed a long time in camps or in prison, people who were tortured or who have lost all their close relatives, who have had to hide in fear for some time, will necessarily be affected in a certain way and may suffer psychological disturbances.[119]

Although no research has been done on the relationship between the specific reasons for the refugees' flight and their settlement it can be assumed that this element will influence their behaviour in the process of settlement. For instance, the clearly political refugees and the mere victims of generalized violence do not share the same views and attitudes and it is probable that they will react in different ways to exile. In this respect the importance of their projected return acquires special significance and has a strong impact on their readiness to adapt in a new country.

Refugees' expectations are also important. The image refugees have formed of the country of settlement and what they expect from it may create either a positive attitude or the risk of disappointment, which will influence the process of settlement.

To this list should be added the specific characteristics of individuals and the length of their stay in the country of settlement. Indeed, psychologists have described the phases that many refugees traverse after their arrival, which include an initial period of mourning characterized by an inability and a refusal to integrate and which is concluded (for most refugees) by the building of a new life in the country of settlement.[120]

External factors
Factors which are more collective and external also have to be considered. The economic and political situation in the host society will to an extent determine how easy it is to find employment and what sympathy will be extended to them. For example, settlement provisions for housing, education, vocational training, health etc. are extremely important.

The existence of historical links between the country of origin and the country of reception as well as the cultural proximity between the two can facilitate the process of settlement and help the learning of the language. On the other hand, cultural distance is likely to aggravate feelings of isolation and alienation.[121]

Refugees who find an established community of compatriots in the host society can sometimes rely on it for support, practical advice and networks (unless contradictions are too great between the first and subsequent groups), as these have acquired the 'know-how' necessary to function in the new society.

Finally, the status and rights enjoyed by refugees, compounded by the length of procedures, will undoubtedly affect the process of settlement. An asylum-seeker who waits for a decision on his status and is not allowed to work or enjoy social rights in the meantime (this may

last several years) is likely to experience a more difficult process of settlement than someone who immediately enjoys Convention status
and the concomitant facilities.

Institutions, policies and issues

Several institutions have a role to play in the settlement of refugees
and, depending on circumstances, they may interrelate more or less
amicably, sometimes enter into conflict, or simply ignore one another.

On the whole governments, albeit inevitably concerned, have taken
few direct responsibilities in settlement other than a financial contribution. A few, such as those in the **Netherlands**, **Sweden**, and in one
case in **Spain**, have managed the reception of refugees in organized
programmes. The Dutch government organized and managed reception centres after NGOs refused to handle them in 1981, and in Spain
the reception of a quota of Indochinese refugees was organized under
the auspices of the Ministry of Labour. Refugee settlement falls within
the remit of a few ministries which are not the same in different countries: the *Centro Regional de Segurança Social de Lisboa in Portugal*; the
Ministry of Labour and Social Security in Spain; the Ministry of
Immigration in Sweden; and several ministries (Social Security, Foreign
Affairs, Interior Ministry) in France.

More often than not the central government has handed over total
or partial responsibility for the settlement of refugees to NGOs which
it supports financially: this is the case in **France**, **Spain**, **Denmark**,
Switzerland, **the UK**, **Italy**, **Belgium**, and **Norway**. This pattern has
increased the discrepancies in provision as NGOs have different methods and approaches. In **France**, for instance, the NGOs divide their
responsibilities: *la Croix Rouge* looks after reception at airports and
takes care of unaccompanied minors; *la Cimade* organizes language
classes; and *France Terre d'Asile* takes charge of housing.[122] In the **UK**,
on the other hand, the division has been territorial: in the case of
refugees from Vietnam, for instance, the Ockenden Venture, Refugee
Action and the British Refugee Council divided responsibilities by
regions.

Compared to the often reluctant involvement of governments, the
involvement of NGOs has been positive, offering greater flexibility and
frequently more commitment. In addition, they have been shown to
organize settlement at far less cost than would have been the case if it
were organized by the government. In some cases established NGOs
have been criticized for limiting their work to recognized refugees,[123]
but this practice is no longer widespread and, in any case, alternative

organizations have been created which do not discriminate between categories of refugees.

Two negative aspects of NGO work can be cited: some lack of professionalism, for which goodwill cannot always compensate,[124] and occasional rivalry between agencies which does not work in the refugees' interest. Results are most positive when there is regular liaison among the various NGOs and between NGOs and other agencies. NGOs also have a subsidiary role as pressure groups on the issue of asylum and settlement policies.[125]

NGOs may be involved in the first stages of settlement and thereafter hand over responsibility for the refugees to local government authorities. In every country there is a point where local authorities have a role to play, although the timing varies. In **Denmark** refugees whose asylum applications have been approved come under the Danish Refugee Council and their transfer to local authorities takes place 18 months later.

In some cases local government bodies take an active role in the resettlement: in **Sweden** and the **Netherlands** they are funded for this purpose. In many countries, for instance in the **UK**, lack of specific funding has made local authorities reluctant to devote resources to refugees, whose needs are frequently ignored. More dramatically, in **Belgium** some municipalities took illegal action in refusing to register refugees on the grounds that it placed too great a burden on them.[126] As a result, refugees were unable to get medical care, send their children to school or receive social assistance.

A major concern is the lack of information and training for local government employees who have to deal with refugees. The Council of Europe Standing Conference of Local and Regional Authorities of Europe (SCLRAE) drew up recommendations on the treatment of refugees, in particular regarding appropriate training for local authority officers. It also recommended the nomination of a specific local executive officer in each authority to take charge of the issues relating to refugees.[127]

Another set of institutions with a role to play in the process of settlement are refugee associations. Refugees have demonstrated a great ability to reconstitute their communities and have created associations that perform a variety of functions. They organize cultural activities ranging from Chilean concerts to Vietnamese New Moon festivals. They advise people in their dealings with the reception society and act as mediators. They constitute pressure groups. They maintain links with the society of origin and reproduce that society. They prepare their people for eventual return to their country. NGO workers or local authority officers often rely on them to communicate with refugees.

UNHCR summarized the central role played by refugee organizations in five vital areas: they help new arrivals with practical matters relating to integration; they provide psychological and material support; they help refugees maintain their cultural identity; they promote a positive image among nationals of the host countries through cultural presentations; and they provide an opportunity for meaningful activity, enhancing the self-image of refugees.[128] As a result SCLRAE recommended that local authorities promote the creation of local and regional associations of refugees and cooperate with them.[129]

These initiatives have been widely welcomed, but there is a need for greater understanding of the settlement process and for policies which reflect this. A number of central issues must be clarified if further progress is to be made.

1. Jewish refugees from Germany are given refuge in Belgium, 1939.
THE HULTON-DEUTSCH COLLECTION

2. Displaced Croatians in Austria with British soldier in 1946.
THE HULTON-DEUTSCH COLLECTION

3. Hungarian refugee children who had fled to Yugoslavia after the failure of the Hungarian uprising of 1956, repatriated to Hungary, 1957. THE HULTON-DEUTSCH COLLECTION

4. Chilean refugees in the UK, at a cultural evening, 1979. DANIÈLE JOLY

5. Kampuchean refugees resettled in family groups, Switzerland, 1982.
A.EGGER/UNHCR

6. Refugee Chilean folk group *Mayapi* (*'Unity'* in Qechua),
London, 1988. LOUIS JARAMILLO

7. 'Refugees in orbit' – this asylum seeker from Iran has spent two years in Roissy Airport, Paris, mid-1980s. ALAIN BUU/FRANK SPOONER PICTURES

8. Ethnic Hungarian refugees from Romania, in Hungary, 1989.
JEAN GAUMY/MAGNUM

9. Vietnamese refugee tailor in the Netherlands, 1989. VERENIGING

10. Somali refugee woman at English-language class organized by the Somali community, London 1990. HOWARD DAVIES/PANOS

11. Iranian refugees protesting at the expulsion of 12 Iranians from France to Gabon, Paris 1987. GILLES BASSIGNAC/GAMMA

12. Kurdish asylum seekers on hunger strike for the right to remain in the UK, London 1992. JON WALTER/KATZ PICTURES

13. Refugees arriving in Hungary from the civil war in Yugoslavia, December 1991. A.HOLLMANN/UNHCR

14. Albanian asylum seekers arriving at Brindisi in Italy, March 1991.
ELIGIO PAONI/KATZ PICTURES

15. Eritrean refugees in the Netherlands, 1989. GOEDELE MONNENS/VLUCHTELINGENWERK

16. Vietnamese refugee children resettled in the UK, 1990. HOWARD DAVIES/PANOS

8

REFUGEE SETTLEMENT: SPECIFIC POLICIES

'Everyone has the right to a standard of living adequate for the health and well-being of himself and of his family, including food, clothing, housing and medical care and necessary social services, and the right to security in the event of unemployment, sickness, disability, widowhood, old age or other lack of livelihood in the circumstances beyond his control.'

– Article 25(1), UN Universal Declaration of Human Rights.

On average, refugees have to wait over a year for a decision which will allow them to settle. But for the individual asylum-seeker the process of settlement begins on arrival. This, however, is not the view of the authorities who want to differentiate between those who will be given permission to stay and those who will not.

Moreover, many countries have deliberately created poor conditions in the pre-asylum period in order to deter asylum-seekers. This policy is maintained in spite of the length of the waiting period and in the knowledge that it is detrimental to the eventual settlement of those who are accepted, thus increasing the burden on the receiving society.[130]

UNHCR and the refugee agencies feel that it is particularly important that asylum-seekers should be allowed to work as soon as possible after they have submitted their application.[131] Once again, whether and when an asylum-seeker is able to work varies throughout Europe.

Reception centres

In most European countries, reception centres exist in one form or another. These centres may occupy a motley collection of premises – old hospitals, hostels or even disused barracks. Opinions are divided as to their desirability and on the optimum length of stay. It has been argued that they are useful because they do not leave people isolated, make it easier to distribute the necessary provisions, and allow for a medical check. They are also a relatively cheap mode of reception.

Against this it is claimed that centres isolate people from society by creating an artificial environment, and may develop a dependency syndrome in their residents if the length of stay is prolonged.[132] In **Belgium**, where refugees are meant to reside one month in the Petit Château reception centre, they often stay up to six months in over-crowded and unsatisfactory conditions. In the **Netherlands**, three months was supposed to be the maximum period but people remain far longer; and in the **UK** refugees from Vietnam stayed for as long as a year in centres.[133]

Another objection to reception centres is that mutually hostile communities may be housed together. In **Spain** one group had to be moved when Laotians and Vietnamese were housed in the same centre.[134] However, this is not always the case, as demonstrated in the **UK** centres at Langtry Walk and Basle Court, both in London, where multi-ethnic communities have interacted well.

Housing

As a basic need, housing is a central issue. But, as in other areas, there is no agreed policy or practice. Generous provision is made for public or subsidized housing in some countries. Refugees are provided with a good deal of subsidized housing in **Scandinavia**, and in the **Netherlands** 5% of all new dwellings built with government subsidies are set aside annually for refugees.[135] On the other hand, in **Belgium** housing has to be found in the private sector. More commonly there is a combination of the two systems, as is the case in **France** and the **UK**, where housing associations have played a central role in providing housing for refugees. In most instances accommodation is not easy to obtain rapidly, and this is frequently a cause of prolonged stays in reception camps.

The allocation of accommodation immediately raises other questions such as the geographical location and distribution of the refugees. In **Belgium** a 'distribution plan' has been approved by the *Conseil des Ministres* establishing criteria for determining how many asylum-seekers should be allocated to particular municipalities. The criteria include the ratio of inhabitants to the national population, the relative prosperity of the municipality, and the number of asylum-seekers already assisted. This plan has, however, been partly held in check by the refusal of some municipalities to accept additional refugees.[136]

Another approach has been the dispersal policy used in the **UK** for the settlement of the Vietnamese. The government and the relevant NGOs agreed that no more than ten and no fewer than four families should be housed in the same municipality, despite the fact that the refugees themselves often expressed the wish to be housed near a 'Vietnamese community'.[137] The rationale behind this decision was that it would not overburden any single local authority and would facilitate local support; it would avoid the creation of ghettoes and a possible backlash on the part of local populations. Ten years later the Vietnamese refugees have regrouped in a few large centres – London, Birmingham and Manchester.

In **Sweden**, Vietnamese refugees have congregated in the Helsingborg-Malmö area where the presence of a Vietnamese community has made Vietnamese food, medicine and videos available.[138] This pattern of secondary migration is confirmed by studies of refugees in the USA and Canada and indicates a need to develop policies which will take account of refugees' wishes to remain together as a community.

However, if refugees are to be concentrated, the local authorities concerned will expect financial support to enable them to provide appropriate services. In the **Netherlands**, this approach has been tried with so-called 'nuclear' municipalities. In **Sweden**, some municipalities were asked to 'specialize' in certain ethnic groups of refugees and given a financial incentive to do so, with the result that it has become easier to provide adequately trained staff and sufficient resources. A study of local and regional authorities concludes that the most desirable model is the concentration of refugees in medium-sized cities. A significant benefit is that refugee communities can provide support to their members, particularly in the case of relatively homogeneous groups. An original project of housing a group of 500 Hmong and another group of 400 Hmong in **French Guiana** (South America) has shown good results.[139]

In some cases refugees themselves have taken positive steps to regroup. There is evidence that Chilean political parties made efforts to concentrate their members geographically and, in at least one significant case, a Vietnamese Catholic priest created the basis for a community to be formed in Birmingham in the UK.

Employment

It is possible that an overriding concern for providing housing will result in more serious longer- term problems by placing obstacles in the way of finding employment. As a rule accommodation is easier to find in areas where unemployment is high. And employment is arguably the most important single factor in successful settlement. It has been claimed that a refugee unable to find a job within a year of arrival could be 'disabled for life'.[140]

But it is not an easy question to resolve. Refugees face major hurdles in trying to break into employment. One problem, for example, is that, paradoxically, one needs to have a job in order to obtain one; an employer's reference is generally required and a positive curriculum vitae is necessary for an application to be successful.

Professional people often cannot practise because there is no equivalence of degrees and qualifications, and they experience severe downward social mobility. In addition, an appropriate language course is required as professional work usually demands mastery of the host country's language. In some cases additional training is required to adapt expertise to a new system and new idiosyncrasies. Arrangements of this kind were made in **France** for Latin American social workers.[141]

In other cases not being a national of the country makes it impossible to enter certain professions such as school teaching in **France**, **Portugal**, **Spain** or **Germany**. In some instances legislation governing employment has been modified to take into account the specific situation of refugees. In **France**, the rule limiting a non-national university lecturer's contract to three years has been waived for Convention refugees.

Manual workers are not so dependent on language skills but they may find that their specific skill is not needed in Europe. Their greatest problem is the discrimination experienced by refugees, especially if they come from the Third World. They frequently have to accept the most menial and worst paid jobs.

Although no accurate statistics are available, it is safe to say that a good number of refugees have had to take up casual undeclared employment – in house cleaning, decorating, childcare and catering. Occasionally refugees succeed in moving on to regular and stable jobs and this has a value beyond its monetary reward; as one refugee said when this happened, it was as though he had regained his dignity.

There is some evidence that local contacts and initiatives yield the best results in providing employment opportunities.[142] Employment schemes developed by refugee workers with local employers have proved positive. In the **Netherlands** strong ties were established between training schemes and local employers; in the **UK** a refugee association in Birmingham has obtained funding for an employment development officer who builds up contacts with local employers; in **France** the *centres d'hébergement* have created useful links with local employers and even launched or supported job creation schemes.[143]

Self-employment projects are another possible avenue. In the south of **France** successful rural projects have been set up.[144] In **Spain** a government programme provides facilities and financial support for refugees who want to start a business or work on the land.[145] A few enterprises of this kind have proved successful in the **UK** and in **France** in the shape of restaurants and craft shops. In the UK these started as cooperatives with loans from Industrial Common Ownership Finance Limited – a government body for the support of workers' cooperatives – and a grant from the county council. Many other examples can be found in European countries.[146]

Training schemes have sometimes led to employment, but they have also failed because they were not tailored to the needs of the trainees. A major obstacle is language. In **Germany** a combination of language training and preparation for work has had positive results. In **Switzerland** a welfare organization has run successful training, work and language programmes since 1982.

Vocational training has to be handled with care. It can cause greater problems than unemployment if it does not lead to jobs. On the whole the employment market is difficult even for nationals and more so for refugees. A good understanding of the local employment situation is necessary; courses have to match local labour demands and be relevant to refugee needs.

As ever, de facto refugees and asylum-seekers encounter the greatest difficulties. Generally they have fewer entitlements than Convention refugees. Their uncertain status arouses suspicion amongst employers, who are further discouraged by the administrative complications and delays in obtaining work permits.

Language and education

Language is crucial to successful settlement. For young people it is the key to access to education; for adults it opens up a wide range of possibilities, not the least of which is managing everyday life.

In all European countries children of refugees – with some exceptions for asylum-seekers – have access to free and compulsory education in schools where they are also taught the host country's language. In some countries the children can be placed in introduction classes before being integrated into the normal courses.

It is too often assumed that children settle into European schools without problems. Several studies indicate that things are not so straightforward.[147] Refugee children would benefit if teachers were given appropriate training and information on their situation and culture. They themselves need an explanation of the 'new system', which they may find very different from their previous experience.

For adults the difficulties are even greater and the available opportunities vary considerably throughout Europe. In **Germany** adult refugees can attend free language classes for nine or 12 months according to their needs; in **Denmark** they have daily language classes of four hours for between six and ten months, and attendance is a condition for obtaining welfare benefits. In **France** and the **Netherlands** refugees are offered respectively 240 hours and 400 hours of lessons.[148] In the **UK** refugees have not been offered special language courses except for those provided for Vietnamese in reception camps, and where courses have been set up through local initiatives.

But even in countries where language courses are organized they do not necessarily meet the needs of the refugees who are not simply learning a new language but also how to function in a different society and culture.[149] In addition, the heterogeneity of the students impedes satisfactory tuition: there is a wide range of languages of origin and people who are illiterate are frequently placed in the same classes as those with a higher level of education, whereas different methods of teaching should obviously be addressed to such disparate groups of people.

Other kinds of education are also important. Where training or courses are offered, grants may have to be given to enable refugees to attend, especially if they have the responsibility of a family. In the **UK** the World University Service (WUS) awards numerous grants to refugees; in **France** refugees have enjoyed the statutory grants available to nationals as well as specific schemes.[150] But first the problem of language has to be resolved.

Insufficient knowledge of the language is a recurrent obstacle for vocational training, further education or obtaining better employment. One aspect of education often mentioned by refugees is the possibility of preparing for a career that may be useful on their return to their own country. WUS and *Cimade* have offered 'development-oriented' grants for this purpose.

Health and social assistance

In most European countries refugees have the same welfare rights as nationals; this is not the case for asylum-seekers and de facto refugees whose rights are more limited and vary greatly from one country to the next. Refugees sometimes also receive additional assistance during the initial period of settlement. Such assistance is currently given in **France, Germany, Luxembourg** and the **Scandinavian countries**.[151]

Social service provision is characterized by the practitioners' lack of training and knowledge. SCLRAE has made strong and wide-ranging recommendations on this issue.[152] Training refugees to become social workers appears to have had positive results in ensuring the delivery of services.[153]

Health issues have to be given far greater attention. Many refugees have gone through deeply traumatic experiences and require sensitive and prolonged counselling. This is compounded by having lost the social world to which they belonged. A good programme, which explains and demystifies the society of settlement, combined with conditions which encourage the preservation of an ethnic community, have been shown to make a positive contribution to mental health.[154]

It is important to make a distinction between mental illness and psychological and behavioural problems. A UNHCR study on the mental health of refugees in five European countries demonstrated the inappropriateness of responses to non-European refugees. Several proposals were put forward to remedy this including the following: the greater involvement of family and refugee associations' networks; the formation of a specialized organization of practitioners focusing on the condition of refugees and on different cultures; and good information on what services were available.[155]

SCLRAE recommends the creation of medical aid centres for refugees, with specialists trained to assist in overcoming the effects of traumatic incidents which may occur many years after the refugee has fled.[156] For counselling, good interpreters are essential and in some instances specialized people from the same community have been able to perform this function.

9

REFUGEE RIGHTS: SOCIAL, CULTURAL AND POLITICAL

'Everyone is entitled to all the rights and freedoms set forth in this Declaration, without distinction of any kind, such as race, colour, sex, language, religion, political or other opinion, national or social origin, property, birth or other status.

   Furthermore, no distinction shall be made on the basis of the political, jurisdictional or international status of the country or territory to which a person belongs, whether it be independent, trust, non-self governing or under any other limitation of sovereignty.'

– Article 2, UN Universal Declaration of Human Rights.

The preservation of cultural identity appears to be a positive element in the integration process.[157] In the **Netherlands** grants are made to a few refugee associations. In two countries, **Norway** and **Sweden**, it is legally compulsory to organize the teaching of the language of origin to refugee children. In **France** books have been reprinted in Lao, Vietnamese and Khmer with great success. Where they have not been provided, refugees themselves have organized numerous mother-tongue classes for their children. They have also promoted a wide variety of cultural functions.

Paradoxically, refugees have sometimes been told that they should not get involved in political activities whereas, for many of them, the sole reason for leaving their country was their political involvement. This constitutes a major motivation to continue politics in exile, and to support the parties that have been defeated or outlawed in their homeland. In **France** a prohibition of this type was challenged, and the only limitation which was upheld requires refugees to respect French law in the course of their political activities. In the **UK**, the Asylum Bill included provisions against asylum-seekers' political activities.

Organizations working with refugees have continuously emphasized that refugees need to nurture their links with their homeland and with their communities in other regions or in other countries.[158] Organizations and links could be encouraged not only on local, regional and national levels but also internationally.

Citizenship

UNHCR has proposed that refugees should be given full access to citizenship as a way of fully belonging to, and participating in, the host society without any restriction.[159] Naturalization certainly provides advantages, including access to some professions barred to non-nationals in several European countries (eg. **Portugal, France, Germany**) and the right to political participation.

But there is more involved than convenience. Despite the advantages to be gained, many, if not most, refugees are reluctant to become citizens of the host country or do so only after a long time has elapsed in exile. Several factors shape this attitude, of which the most important is loyalty to the homeland which they were forced to leave.

Public opinion

Refugees are very sensitive to public opinion. The attitude of the surrounding population affects most aspects of their everyday life and it can make the difference between a supportive, harmonious, friendly environment and unpleasant, hostile, prejudiced encounters.

The major agent shaping public opinion is the media. As a rule the media tend to report home rather than international news and to focus on sensational stories, which in practice often means negative ones. As the French saying goes: *'les peuples heureux n'ont pas d'histoire'* ('Happy people have no history'). Positive stories of refugees in the host societies make headline news much less frequently than negative ones. On the other hand, the causes of the refugees' flight are rarely presented accurately or in depth as they are not perceived as relevant to a domestic readership. The false perceptions resulting from this distortion of the refugee story are aggravated by the overwhelmingly hostile statements issued by many politicians, which are then widely covered by the media.

As a result, refugees are increasingly presented not as people in need of protection but as people who are a threat, not as people who *have* a problem but as people who *are* a problem. Large headlines proclaim that 'unjustified claims of refugee status "will not be accepted"',[160] and that there will be 'fines to halt bogus refugees'.[161] This was followed by 'airline fines have cut refugee influx' with an article explaining that...

'The number of immigrants applying for refugee status has fallen rapidly since the government warned airlines they would be fined if they carried passengers without proper documents.'[162] The effect of such reporting is to reinforce the underlying paradigm on which government policies on asylum are based: refugees are first and foremost perceived and presented as undesirables – illegal immigrants, potential terrorists and drug dealers.

To counteract this 'bad press', refugee agencies have organized campaigns of public information in several European countries. In 1988 the **Danish** Youth Federation launched a one-year campaign to promote friendship and tolerance between Danish refugees and immigrants. **French** NGOs organized a Refugee Day in September 1989 as part of the bicentennial celebrations for the French Revolution. The 'Yes to a colourful brotherhood' campaign in **Norway** and a week-long **Swedish** campaign in 1989 promoted the settlement of refugees in municipalities and was followed by a major campaign with the slogan 'Yes, room for humanity'. In 1989, a fourth 'refugee day' was held in **Germany**.

The Council of Europe and UNHCR recommended that local authorities should organize publicity campaigns for refugees. Finally, ECRE warned against the pernicious use of language and recommended that such terms as 'floods', 'influxes', 'torrents', 'streams', 'bogus', 'swamped', etc. should be avoided and a more positive image of refugees promoted.[163]

Return

Return to their country of origin is a central concern for many refugees, and the process of settlement is fundamentally affected by it. A proportion of refugees return when the circumstances that obliged them to leave their homeland have changed: this was the case with Uruguayans, Argentinians, Chileans. It has been shown, however, that unsuccessful settlement frequently leads to unsuccessful returns. In any case, it is seldom an easy process, and refugees themselves have stressed the importance of good preparation.

Refugee organizations have played an active part in these preparations. For example, the *Comisión de Informacion Sobre el Retorno Chileno* in Paris holds weekly sessions of advice for refugees who wish to return home and emphasizes the need for such a service.

Host countries could play a positive role by reaching agreements with the refugees' countries of origin to facilitate their return, particularly in relation to practical matters such as pension arrangements and the restitution of civil rights.

However, refugee agencies insist that it must be ensured at all times that return is voluntary and that no pressure is put on refugees to return against their will. To date, such pressure has not been applied within Europe. When the situation in the refugees' homeland has changed, they have usually been allowed to stay on. In **France**, Argentinians who wished to remain have been given the chance to obtain French nationality, as their refugee status came to an end. But the **UK** has been prepared to force Vietnamese refugees in Hong Kong to return to Vietnam which, taken together with adverse publicity and increasing numbers of refoulement cases, may herald a general change in approach.

Unaccompanied minors

The arrival on their own of children and young people is a relatively new but growing phenomenon which raises a variety of problems. Some are legal, relating to 'personal status' and guardianship. In some cases – **Denmark, Iceland, Norway** and **the UK** – they are decided in relation to the country of domicile; in others – **Germany, France, Italy, Sweden, Switzerland** and **Austria** – on the basis of nationality. A 'minor' is defined as a person under 18 in most European countries.[164]

Decisions on minor asylum-seekers are influenced by government fears that they may open the door for larger movements through family reunion. Finally, the whole area of care and the best way to settle these young people has still to be explored thoroughly. Group accommodation seems to have had positive results in the **UK**, **Sweden** and **Denmark**.

Contributing to society

Good settlement conditions make it easier for refugees to make a positive contribution to their host society. Many do so in a variety of ways. Refugees have become integrated into all the branches of the labour market using skills that they brought with them: Chilean miners have become coal miners in Scotland, Vietnamese tailors and jewellers have continued with their trades. Others have learned new skills: many taxi drivers in Paris are refugees. Professionals – engineers, doctors, academics – have also made their contribution. All adult refugees are potential contributors to their host society, which does not have to bear the cost of their education. And refugees themselves overwhelmingly want to make a contribution.

In a more special way, refugees have also added new dimensions to the culture of the societies which receive them. Evidence of the cultural contribution is provided by the significant number of established artists. There is a growing body of literature written in exile, theatre groups are thriving from the Cypriot Teatro Technis in London to the Chilean theatre Aleph in Paris, while visual artists and a range of musical groups add to the mix.

However, the real impact is in the refugees' way of life. For instance, although a few of the greatest Latin American groups and singers in exile are well known, every Chilean *peña* has its singers and guitarists. In those countries where there are independent radio stations this kaleidoscope of cultures has been broadcast, making it available to all. Restaurants created by refugees have not only provided a place to eat but also opened another part of the world to their hosts.

Refugees have contributed to every walk of life, including the ideological and the political, in the host society. Many have joined trade unions. Others have played an active role in political life: for example one Italian mayor is a Chilean refugee.

Although refugees are opposed to the regimes which have forced them to flee, they act as ambassadors of the people of their country and as representatives of their culture and society. One could argue that they have helped to open minds and combat racism and prejudice.

Of course, not all refugees have been able to make positive contributions. There are problems in finding employment and adapting to a new society which have led to disillusion and apathy. Such cases create an image of refugees as a burden to the society that has settled them. Nevertheless, given the vast difficulties encountered by refugees, it is a testament to their strength and vitality that so many have done so well.

It must be the primary objective of good settlement policies in housing, education, health and employment to create conditions that make it possible for all refugees to contribute equally with the host population to the well-being of society.

10

REFUGEES IN EASTERN EUROPE: AN OVERVIEW

'Everyone has the right to freedom of movement and residence within the borders of each state.

Everyone has the right to leave any country, including his own and to return to his country.'

– Article 13, (1) and (2), UN Universal Declaration of Human Rights.

The background

The aftermath of World War II saw the establishment of Soviet-style communist regimes in Eastern Europe and massive population transfers. The largest of these involved the expulsion and emigration of over 12 million Germans, predominantly from the new Poland (over eight million) and from Czechoslovakia (over two and a half million), and some one and a half million Poles from pre-war Polish territories annexed by the USSR. In addition, some three million Poles and almost two million Czechs and Slovaks were resettled in the areas vacated by the expelled Germans.[165] Many of the Jews who survived the Holocaust emigrated to the new state of Israel.

The impetus for the founding of UNHCR in 1951 was the problem of refugees fleeing communist Eastern Europe and, while the return of these refugees was always an avowed aim, the bloc mentality of the Cold War saw the predominance of curative measures as opposed to preventative ones, resulting in external settlement as opposed to repatriation.[166]

All the new communist governments, with the exception of Albania, eventually ratified the International Covenant on Civil and Political Rights, Article 12 of which guarantees the right of citizens to leave their own country. Of these states only **Yugoslavia** under Tito allowed its citizens to leave freely and in the boom of the 1950s and 1960s large numbers of migrant workers from all over Yugoslavia went to

Western Europe, especially West Germany, in search of lucrative employment. Many remained and settled there. The exodus continued into the 1990s. For example in August 1991 alone, 2579 Slovenes emigrated from Slovenia.[167]

Moreover, within Yugoslavia, the implementation of the 1974 constitution (which created six republics and two autonomous provinces) resulted in many ways in a de facto confederacy, with great variations between the different units.[168] In some instances this led to migration within the country itself akin to emigration. There was a general movement from the impoverished rural south to the more prosperous north. However, the most noticeable migration was the exodus of Serbs from the former autonomous province of Kosovo which is now overwhelmingly inhabited by ethnic Albanians.

Until the momentous changes of the late 1980s, the other Eastern European states pursued extremely restrictive policies to prevent their citizens emigrating. The Berlin Wall, constructed in 1961 to dam the continuous flow from East to West Germany, was both a symbol and an expression of this denial of freedom of movement. However, there were some exceptions. In **Bulgaria** over 150,000 ethnic Turks were allowed, or obliged, to emigrate to Turkey in 1950-1, and a further wave of emigration of ethnic Turks, on the grounds of family reunification, was allowed from 1968 to 1978.[169] In 1956, many refugees fled from **Hungary** after the restoration of the communist status quo by Soviet tanks, and again in 1968 many fled from **Czechoslovakia** after the failure of the 'Prague Spring'. Similarly many Poles fled **Poland** in 1956, 1968 and 1981.

Throughout the 1980s, **Romania** allowed sizeable numbers of its citizens to emigrate to the West. This was permitted primarily for financial reasons connected with the continuance of 'Most Favoured Nation Status' in trading relations with the USA which, under the Jackson-Vannick amendment, was contingent on emigration policy. Such leeway for emigrants from Romania mainly affected ethnic Germans; eg. 14,831 of the 21,200 Romanian citizens who officially emigrated in 1984 were ethnic Germans, allegedly because of an unofficial payment of 10,000DM per person by the West German authorities.[170]

However, these were exceptions to the rule whereby citizens of the Eastern European communist states (except Yugoslavia) were denied permission to emigrate legally and faced severe penalties if caught attempting to cross the heavily fortified and patrolled borders to the West.

The changes of the late 1980s

The Jaruzelski government in **Poland** was the first to allow large numbers of its citizens to cross legally into Western Europe and soon convoys of Polish cars en route to places as far afield as Istanbul to buy goods became commonplace. Many of these people took advantage of the new situation and left Poland on tourist visas to Western European states with the intention of settling there. In addition to such primarily economic motives, pressure for emigration was strongly connected with the situation regarding minorities within the region – especially that of ethnic Hungarians in Romania and ethnic Turks in Bulgaria.

In 1988-9 the deteriorating situation in **Romania** under the dictatorial rule of Nicolae Ceausescu resulted in the unprecedented situation of thousands of citizens of one communist regime – Romania – fleeing and applying for asylum in another – **Hungary**. Initially the vast majority of these were ethnic Hungarians but by the summer of 1989 the proportion of ethnic Romanians had risen to over 25%.[171] At the same time, the forced assimilation policy of the Zhivkov regime in **Bulgaria** resulted in a mass exodus of up to 350,000 ethnic Turks, predominantly to Turkey.[172]

The pace of change dramatically accelerated with large numbers of would-be emigrants from **East Germany** seeking refuge in embassies in **Hungary** and **Czechoslovakia**. The Hungarian authorities, who were in the process of dismantling the Leninist state from the top, appeared to be unwilling to continue the past practice of forcibly preventing citizens from their erstwhile communist allies, especially East Germany, from crossing their borders illegally. These refugees were a major factor in the downfall of the East German regime and the subsequent dismantling of the Berlin Wall.

By the end of 1989, the momentous changes had swept aside all the governments of COMECON (Council for Mutual Economic Assistance) Eastern Europe. Indeed, 1989 was a momentous year for population movements from Eastern Europe. Approximately 1.3 million people were involved: 720,000 Germans from **East Germany** and other states moved to **West Germany**; up to 350,000 ethnic Turks left **Bulgaria** mostly for Turkey; 140,000 Soviet Jews departed for Israel; along with 80,000 other Eastern Europeans (mostly Poles moving to Western Europe).[173]

Apart from East Germany, which voted for unification with West Germany and thus ceased to exist, the new state authorities, whether non-communist (Poland, Hungary, Czechoslovakia) or ex-communist (Bulgaria and Romania), all introduced liberalization and freedom of movement and sought a close relationship with Western Europe. This meant that both the reasons for refugee flight from East to West and the attitudes of Western European states to asylum-seekers from the East changed dramatically.

In 1970 there were 13,000 asylum-seekers in Western Europe, most of whom came from Eastern Europe, virtually all of whom were recognized as genuine asylum cases. In 1990, the number of applicants for asylum was approximately 450,000, of whom fewer than 20% were recognized as refugees and of whom only about 50% were from former COMECON Eastern Europe. Most new refugees from the East now originated from Turkey and Yugoslavia.[174]

Despite the drop in percentage terms of Eastern European asylum applicants, their numbers have risen greatly, whilst their chances of recognition have dropped dramatically as the Eastern European states have changed their restrictive policies on human rights.

An overview

Poland, **Hungary**, **Bulgaria** and **Czechoslovakia** have all joined the Council of Europe and **Romania** holds special status there, with future membership probable. **Yugoslavia** also possessed special status and the new successor states (**Croatia**, **Slovenia** etc.) emerging from the old Yugoslav state are likely at various times in the near future also to gain this status, leading to eventual membership. **Albania** is also likely to become a member.

All Eastern European countries have declared their willingness to accede to the 1951 UN Convention, and **Hungary**, **Poland** and **Czechoslovakia** have already signed, although Hungary maintained the geographical reservation which excludes non-Europeans. There are now UNHCR offices in all Eastern European countries.

The situation today is different from the post-war period, which produced relatively clear-cut cases of individual refugees fleeing communist state persecution. The basic root causes for leaving are now the economic disparity between Western and Eastern Europe, relative or severe poverty and a desire to 'see the world'. However, unemployment and political and social tension may again lead to mass emigration. Three main categories of mass migration are emerging.

The first is the continuation of current migration by particular ethnic groups, especially minority groups who feel insecure, even if they do not face political persecution. Two groups which fall into this category are the ethnic Germans who are found in most Eastern European states and Russia, and the Jews who are a minority everywhere.

The second arises from persecution of particular ethnic or social groups such as Gypsies (Roma), and from internal disturbances, most notably the civil war in the former territories of Yugoslavia. In several Eastern European states Roma, with their distinctive appearance, way of life and, sometimes also, religion, have provided a readily available scapegoat and focus for old prejudices and new frustrations. The war between Serbia, under the guise of the Yugoslav state, and Croatia was unprecedented in European post-war history, and resulted in large-scale displacement of populations.

The most common reason for mass migration is likely to be economic in origin. This may take a more dramatic form than at present, due to a collapse in the economies in Eastern Europe leading to a flight from poverty akin to the 'south to north' movements. It is noticeable that at the present time the bulk of Eastern European migrants are from the less developed, more unstable Balkans – Romania, Bulgaria and Albania as well as war-torn Yugoslavia – rather than the more developed 'northern tier' countries of Hungary and Czechoslovakia. However, Poland, because of its economic problems and also because of its German minority living in the border lands adjacent to Germany, also figures highly in terms of migrant numbers.

To date, the great fear commonly voiced in early 1991 of a massive influx of refugees from the East, caused by the possible violent disintegration of the USSR, has not occurred but the potential for such an influx remains. Such problems of transient refugees are most acute in the 'frontline' Eastern European states of **Hungary**, **Poland** and **Czechoslovakia** where transient asylum-seekers have arrived, hoping to cross into Western Europe but having been denied permission. In these three states the pressures arising from this new situation are forcing the authorities to tighten up on illegal immigration.

Yet by early 1992 the single greatest source of refugees and displaced peoples in Europe derived from the violent break-up of the Yugoslav state and the creation in its wake of a number of smaller states, some with enclaves and border areas effectively under the control of outside governments and military forces. It is unlikely that the scale of the violence and displacement in the Balkans will be repeated elsewhere; nevertheless further possible fragmentation in the ex-USSR and Czechoslovakia, raises vital questions on the boundaries of the new Europe and how these are likely to affect asylum-seekers.

11

EASTERN EUROPE: REFUGEES IN THE 1990S

*'The consolidation of nation-states – both in the case of republics enter-
ing into a new union and particularly in the case of leaving the USSR –
must not allowed to be accompanied by any infringement of the rights
of the minorities...However it is not only our own experience: if Europe
does not wish to be confronted by a flood of refugees, with armed conflicts, inter-ethnic hatred, it must keep a very strict watch on the observance of minority rights by all subject states in its space. Otherwise the
whole European process will collapse, burying human rights, too, in
its wake.'*

– Mikhail Gorbachev, (former) President of the USSR, addressing
CSCE Human Rights Conference, Moscow, 10 September 1991.

Target countries for population movements

Of all the countries in Eastern Europe, **Hungary**, because of its proximity both to the West and to the civil conflict between Serbs and Croats in Yugoslavia, and because of the large number of ethnic Hungarians living in neighbouring states, faces the greatest diversity of refugee-related problems. Ironically, how-ever, after Hungary introduced greater freedom of travel for its own cit-izens in the 1980s, emigration from the country declined and Hungary instead became a target country.

The influx began in 1987. By early 1991 over 50,000 had arrived, of whom 85% were from Romania and of these 80% were ethnic Hungarians.[175] Ethnic Hungarians from the USSR also figured in these numbers. Over 35,000 of the refugees received assistance from the Hungarian Red Cross which, from August to September 1989, also assisted some 40,000 East Germans.[176]

Between 1968 and 1989, 244,597 people left **Czechoslovakia**.[177] Since then mass emigration has not occurred, mainly because of the

75

country's relative economic stability and potential for development. Moreover, Czechoslovakia does not face the same magnitude of possible immigration of native-speakers or those with historic ties to the state as does Hungary.

At a press conference in March 1992, it was announced that 625 of 3250 applicants had been granted refugee status. Of these, 44% were Romanian citizens, 17% Bulgarians, 13% from the former USSR and 3% were Vietnamese citizens who remained in Czechoslovakia after their work contracts expired.[178]

Poland suffers greater economic problems than either Hungary or Czechoslovakia and this has been reflected in the greater numbers of emigrants from the country in recent years. Nor has it attracted either asylum-seekers or immigrants. Most have preferred to go elsewhere.

In the summer of 1990 several hundred asylum-seekers from Third World countries were turned back by the Swedish authorities after trying to cross to Sweden from Poland. These people had no formal status, as Poland had not at that stage signed the 1951 Convention, but they were cared for by the authorities, initially near the port of Swinoujscie and then later relocated to health resorts near Warsaw.[179]

Such asylum-seekers generally were not happy to remain in Poland and most eventually left for other countries. In May 1991 it was announced that there were about 330 asylum-seekers registered in Poland of whom 298 had been granted refugee status and 32, mostly Lithuanians, refused status by UNHCR.[180]

In addition to **Germany**, two other EC countries have become target countries for a specific group of asylum-seekers from Eastern Europe. Thousands of Albanians have attempted to escape the country's acute economic problems, resulting in a massive wave of Albanian emigration to **Greece** and **Italy**.

Before this massive influx of Albanian citizens, **Greece** had had few refugees in recent times. Those who registered with UNHCR, often left-wing Turks fleeing repression in Turkey, were housed at the Lavrion refugee camp outside Athens. A number of refugees from the Horn of Africa arrived at the end of the 1980s and could be seen sleeping rough in Athens. In March 1991 there were reports that the government planned to settle several thousand Pontians, ethnic Greeks from the former USSR, in the Rodopi province in the north where the majority of the population are Muslims (ethnic Turks and Greek- and Bulgarian-speaking Muslims).[181]

Yugoslavia also became a target country for Albanian refugees, although on a much smaller scale than Italy or Greece. Some 300 ethnic Macedonians fled to Yugoslav Macedonia in March 1991[182] and many more presumably followed. Over 1000 refugees from Albania were registered in Montenegro by late January 1992.[183] By February, Yugoslavia had returned 411 asylum-seekers to Albania.[184]

Bulgaria has attracted few refugees as such, although ethnic Bulgarians from the former USSR remain a potential source of refugees or immigrants, particularly if serious disturbances were to occur in the successor states. Ivan Dundarov, chairperson of the Union of Bessarabian and Tauric Bulgarians, told a news conference on 12 March 1992 that the 700,000 Bulgarians of the former USSR, most of whom have retained contact with relatives in Bulgaria, want to return. The union has requested 150,000 hectares of state and municipal land formerly belonging to their ancestors for this purpose and is awaiting a decision from the Bulgarian authorities.[185]

There have also been a few applicants for asylum in **Romania**. The Romanian government decided to allot some funds for the temporary stay of refugees but their legal status was not clear and in June 1991 the government was awaiting a UNHCR decision as to status.[186] Until the break-up of the USSR in December 1991, Romania had a bilateral agreement to return Soviet asylum-seekers. Refugee issues were handled by three different ministries, the Interior, Foreign Affairs and Justice, with the result that matters were often mishandled or not dealt with at all.

Countries producing mass population movement

Before the political changes of 1991, few Albanians managed to leave the country, legally or as refugees. Since that time poverty, mass unemployment and the breakdown of public order have spurred hundreds of thousands of people, especially young men, into attempting to leave **Albania** in the hopes of a better life abroad. Few could be considered as refugees under the UNHCR Convention and in practice nearly all have been treated as illegal economic immigrants.

Most Albanians have initially headed for Greece or Italy, which are geographically close and where they have some ethnic or historic links, although some hoped ultimately to reach the richer northern European countries. Despite mass repatriation from both Greece and Italy, there appears to be no immediate end to pressure to emigrate. On 11 January 1992 a crowd of over 1000 'bent on exodus' gathered near the port of Vlore and battled with the police.[187]

Bulgaria faces emigration on such a scale as possibly to seriously damage the country's development. Apart from the exodus of ethnic Turks, huge numbers of Slav Bulgarians have also left the country following the relaxation of travel regulations after the fall of Todor Zhivkov in November 1989. From May to June 1989 some 138,000 were officially noted as having emigrated. However, Professor Minko Minkov[188] calculates the true number as reaching 400,000, most of whom were young people.

There was also some inward movement. By the end of 1991 perhaps half of the 350,000 ethnic Turks had returned from Turkey (the Anatolian News Agency gave a figure of 235,000).[189] Some 2500 ethnic Turks also fled to Sweden, but following the relaxation in Bulgaria, the Swedish government decided to deport them back to Bulgaria.

Many of the returnees from Turkey effectively became refugees in their own country of origin as many had sold, or were obliged to sell, their houses at reduced rates to obtain passports. Some even returned to find that their homes had been destroyed – in Haskovo local officials had ordered the destruction of over 1000 homes – even though officially they had left on tourist passports with three-month visas.[190] Over a thousand people started hunger strikes in protest and in April 1991 the Justice Minister announced that 2080 such housing complaints had been lodged, with 1035 already considered and the claims found to be justified.[191] In August 1991 he announced that a compensation fund of 170-80m. *leva* was planned for all ethnic Turks who had returned to find their properties confiscated or destroyed.[192]

Despite the many who returned, disillusioned with life in Turkey, many thousands continued to emigrate there: 6000 a month in early 1990.[193] Some 200 Pomaks (Islamicized Slavs) went to the Greek border in early 1991 to try to emigrate to Greece, apparently without success.

Following the overthrow of Ceausescu in December 1989, **Romania** also liberalized its laws on freedom of movement and huge numbers have taken advantage of this to emigrate. Political instability, economic deterioration and ethnic discrimination have exacerbated this emigration, many ethnic Hungarians having moved to Hungary as they will continue to do in the immediate future.

Interior Ministry statistics for 1990 state that some 130,000 applications for residence abroad were approved, with an ethnic breakdown of 95,671 Germans, 17,782 Romanians, 13,210 Hungarians, 1289 Jews, and 1762 other nationalities.[194] These figures are only for those who officially applied for residence abroad. Many others left the country on normal passports; over three and a half million were issued and some 400,000 others were being processed at the end of 1990 alone.[195] Reports in the Romanian media of 800,000 Romanian citizens having emigrated in the first eight months of 1990 were dismissed by the government as exaggerated.[196]

All agree that the bulk of emigrants appear to be men between the ages of 20 and 35, many of whom are well educated. For example, 77% of the asylum-seekers in Switzerland were from Romania, the majority of them ethnic Romanians. Most of this group were single (60%), from big cities (35% from Bucharest and only 8% from the countryside) and well educated.[197] The inference is clear: Romania, along with Bulgaria and Albania, is in danger of losing its intelligentsia by emigration.

Minorities and special groups

Ethnic Germans

Poland has a sizeable ethnic German minority which for many years was officially viewed as being smaller than in fact it was. There has been a thriving black market in forged papers allowing Poles to claim German ancestry and thus German citizenship. In 1990 the police estimated that some 30,000 Poles had thus acquired bogus German nationality and emigrated,[198] and the same source gives the huge figure of 300,000 'ethnic Germans' registered as having left Poland in the period 1988-90. This figure appears inflated but highlights how many Poles have circumvented tighter German controls on immigration.

Huge numbers of ethnic Germans have left **Romania**, with almost 100,000 leaving in 1990 alone. These account for perhaps half the total number of ethnic Germans within Romania. Despite a slowing of this exodus in 1991, there is a real possibility of almost the entire community leaving for Germany unless the economic and political situation improves in Romania.

Roma (Gypsies)

Thousands of **Romanian** Roma have left for the West, especially for Germany. They have caused immense problems for the 'frontline' states of **Hungary**, **Czechoslovakia** and **Poland**. Racism against Roma is widespread in Romania. There were reports of many Roma leaving the country or being expelled during the Ceausescu era.[199] In the post-communist period, there have been many attacks on them by some sections of the population, often in collusion with local officials.

In **Poland** the 15,000 or so Roma population appears to be leaving en masse, aggravated by indigenous racism against them. For example, in the immediate aftermath of the indiscriminate mob attacks on Roma in Mlawa on 26 June 1991, over 1000 fled to Sweden but were turned back by the Swedish authorities.[200] However many succeeded in crossing illegally into Germany.

In addition, Poland is now a major transit point on the illegal Roma emigration route from Romania to **Germany**.[201] Many Roma families from Romania live temporarily on rubbish dumps and in railway stations after being refused entry into Germany, awaiting a chance to cross illegally. German officials reported that during 1991 between 50 and 100 were crossing into Germany each week.[202] German border guards stated that illegal entrants were returned to the Polish authorities who were obliged under a bilateral treaty with Germany to deport them to their country of origin, but the Polish police were not equipped to enforce deportation orders sending Roma back to Romania.[203]

Although these transient Roma qualify for assistance from the Department of Refugees and the Polish Red Cross (PCK), the majority do not wish for such aid and want to cross into Germany as quickly as possible, by illegal means if necessary.

Vietnamese guest workers
A particular problem relates to the large numbers of Vietnamese guest workers who are working in some Eastern European states under agreements made by the former communist authorities and who, in many cases, are loath to return to Vietnam.

In March 1990 in **Czechoslovakia** there were as many as 37,000 Vietnamese whose contracts were expiring. After the government announced that their contracts would not be renewed and they would have to return home, many crossed illegally into Austria – 100 on 21 March alone.[204] In the event, it appeared that total repatriation in so short a time was not feasible and in June 1991 some 29,000 remained, with 10,000 of them due to leave by the end of the year.

However, illegal emigration of Vietnamese continued and in December 1991 the Czechoslovak Interior Ministry announced tougher measures. Vietnamese workers in Czechoslovakia who illegally left the country to apply for asylum in other European states would henceforth forfeit both their work contracts and their residence permits if returned to Czechoslovakia, while former Vietnamese guest workers could only revisit Czechoslovakia with valid tourist visas.[205]

By early 1991 **Bulgaria** had about 20,000 Vietnamese guest workers in the country under arrangements made by the Zhivkov regime. They had come for a maximum stay of five years per person, but it proved relatively easy to stay on by using bribery and other means. A series of violent incidents between Vietnamese and Bulgarian citizens in 1990 and 1991 prompted the authorities to repatriate them as quickly as possible. Some 12,000 remained in June 1991 but it was announced that all would have left Bulgaria by the end of August 1991.[206]

There were 100,000 Vietnamese workers in East Germany in 1989 but most returned to Vietnam on the expiry of their contracts. By early 1992, 20,000 remained, often living in appalling conditions. About 50% have applied for political asylum in unified Germany but only 0.4% have been granted refugee status and in March a north German court ruled that they were 'not political opponents of their government'. The German government offered to provide financial incentives to Vietnamese willing to return voluntarily.[207]

Other ethnic groups

In **Romania**, the 20,000 or so remaining Jews faced an upsurge of anti-semitism and around a thousand left for Israel in the period January to October 1990.[208] The unstable situation in Romania, especially in regard to minorities, even resulted in 500 or so ethnic Ukrainians marching to the border with the Ukraine and threatening to emigrate there in protest – something of an exception to the almost universal East-West movement of migration in Europe.

There has been a trickle of ethnic Czech immigrants from the Chernobyl zone of the Ukraine after it was declared a disaster zone in December 1989. The first 35 such 'environmental refugees' arrived at a civil defence camp in Hodoviz in western Czechoslovakia in May 1991 and more than 1000 were expected to be resettled in villages near the German border by the end of 1991.[210]

12

YUGOSLAVIA: A EUROPEAN REFUGEE CRISIS

'... the solutions can no longer be sought in the old ways – war, conflicts and state hegemonisms... ways forward from Balkan ethnic diversities and ethnic entanglements should only be sought and found, even if it can only be achieved over the long run, in strict implementation of human rights, patient settlement of disputes, in open democratic societies and non-aggressive, non-hegemonistic state policies.'

– Milovan Djilas, Foreword to *Minorities in the Balkans*

Both the scale and the ferocity of the **Yugoslavian** civil war has been unprecedented in post-World War II Europe. From June 1991, when Slovenia and Croatia declared their independence from Yugoslavia, confrontation between the federal authorities, in particular the federal army (JNA), and the rebellious republics has become open civil war. It rapidly evolved into a conflict between Serbia and its supporters in both the federal government and ethnic Serbians in the other republics, and Croatia. This conflict and its ramifications, especially in the ethnically mixed areas of Bosnia-Hercegovina, have resulted in hundreds of thousands of displaced people – estimates range to up to one and a third million.

The financial costs

It was soon apparent that the initial UNHCR budget of $US 24 million allocated to deal with the refugees resulting from the civil war was hopelessly inadequate.[211] At the end of January 1992 it was announced that the cost of the displaced people was over $US 15m. per month. For the moment, most were being supported by their families.

The Yugoslavian federal budget (whatever that term actually meant by this time) for 1992, would provide ten times for relief as did the allocation for 1991 and stated that for the first six months of 1992, displaced people (mainly in Serbia and Bosnia-Hercegovina) would receive six billion dinars ($US 60m.).[212]

In late February, Tanjug announced that the ICRC was to more than double its budget for displaced people in Yugoslavia, from 16 million Swiss Francs in 1991 to approximately 37 million Swiss Francs, and UNHCR would also increase its aid.[213]

In February the Croatian Office for Refugees announced it was spending DM 3m. per day on caring for over 320,000 displaced people. The status of these people would be dealt with by the Department of Foreign Affairs in the Interior Ministry. Until that time they had been granted immediate refugee status but after the international recognition of Croatia their status may or may not be recognized in line with the international covenants.[214]

The EC also sent considerable aid; by March 1992, 1500 tons of wheat flour through UNHCR and $US 50,000 worth of aid for babies in Serbia had been sent through the EC monitor mission and UNICEF in Belgrade.[215]

Displaced peoples in the new republics

The extension of the conflict to Bosnia-Hercegovina seriously aggravated an already acute situation. Although the number of refugees in **Slovenia** from Croatia had decreased from over 20,000, according to the Slovene Red Cross at the end of 1991, to about 5000[216] Slovenia complained in May about the lack of Western help in coping with almost 30,000 refugees of whom 25,000 were from Bosnia-Hercegovina. Some 7232 were accommodated in 32 assembly centres while others were with relatives or friends. In some assembly centres, former JNA facilities, there was fear of possible epidemics due to insanitary conditions. Accommodation, food and medical services were costing Slovenia 100,000 DM per day and the government intimated that 'comprehensive measures' would be put to the assembly to deal with the problem.[217]

The Assistant Interior Minister of Slovenia, Bogo Brvar, said on 27 April that many fleeing Bosnia-Hercegovina were trying to leave Slovenia for Austria but were prevented by Austrian police and sent back. The Interior Minister, Igor Bancar, warned that Slovenia might close her borders to refugees unless the West (Austria and Italy) opened their borders.[218]

In **Croatia** the situation was worse. Over 125,000 refugees from Bosnia-Hercegovina were registered in Croatia by 21 April with more arriving every day, either from the direction towards Zupanja, Samac and Slavonski Brod, or towards Ploce, Metkovic, Makarska and Split.

Aid and aid stocks were said to be dwindling fast and in many places, especially the Dalmatian coast and Slavonija, refugees outnumbered the local inhabitants.[219] On 28 April the Bihac Red Cross office requested emergency food aid from the ICRC to halt starvation of some 45,000 refugees in the area of Cazinska Krajina.[220]

At the end of 1991, with the conflict in Croatia apparently declining, the Red Cross organizations reported, in addition to the 20,000 refugees from Croatia in Slovenia, over 150,000 refugees registered in Serbia, almost 95,000 in Bosnia-Hercegovina, just over 7000 from Croatia in Montenegro, with another 1100 from Albania. In addition, there were about 2300 refugees registered in Macedonia although how many were from the conflict in Croatia and how many from Albania was not clear.[221]

In early 1992 the ICRC, together with what remained of the federal authorities, were attempting to search for people missing as a result of the conflict in Croatia.[222] The Croat government at a news conference on 22 January 1992 stated that there were 322,000 refugees in Croatia – presumably mainly people displaced internally in Croatia as opposed to those coming from other Yugoslav republics.[223]

The leader of the main Hungarian political party in Vojvodina, Andras Agostan, said about 25,000 Hungarians had been forced to flee to Vojvodina either to avoid conscription into the JNA or to avoid atrocities by Serbian para-militaries.[224]

In February the Serb authorities announced that all refugees from Croatia to **Serbia** would be issued with special identity cards without which no financial support or other rights would be forthcoming.[225] In the same month the Serbian Academy announced that, according to a study it had made with the Sociological Agency Forum and the Serbian Office of Statistics, up to 40% of Serbs who had fled Croatia for Serbia or Bosnia-Hercegovina did not want to return.[226]

On 1 April the Serbian Assembly passed a law covering the 166,000 or so refugees from Croatia in Serbia. It envisaged the Commission for Refugees would take charge of refugee accommodation and decide on the granting of or rescinding of refugee status.[227]

The spread of fighting in March to **Bosnia-Hercegovina** with its intricately mixed populations of Muslims, Serbs and Croats, and the ensuing bitter inter-communal fighting has further inflated these already high figures for displaced people. On 4 May the Serb Red Cross said that there were now 243,289 refugees in Serbia, of whom 73,975 were registered from Bosnia-Hercegovina, and new arrivals every day. The violence in Sarajevo had also caused a fresh wave of refugees to Montenegro where the total was now 14,227.[228]

The self-styled government of the so-called Serbian Republic of Bosnia-Hercegovina claimed the huge figure of some 200,000 Serbs having fled from Bosnia-Hercegovina. They claim some 80,000 Serbs have fled from Sarajevo alone (Sarajevo's population at the last census was about 600,000 residents of whom about a third were Serbs), about 40,000 from the Sava river valley, and over 30,000 from the Neretva valley.[229]

On the other hand, UNHCR estimated a total of 400,000 refugees from Bosnia-Hercegovina, of whom almost 122,000 are still in the republic with some 201,000 in Croatia.[230]

Population transfers

Whether such people will eventually return to their homes if and when the situation stabilizes is uncertain. It is likely that many will not, especially Serbs or Croats who previously lived in areas dominated by a majority from the other group and where severe atrocities were carried out. Nor perhaps will many of the ethnic Hungarians who fled to Hungary.

Conversely it appears that the Serbs are deliberately settling Serb refugees in places vacated by Croats and Hungarians who fled when the areas fell under Serbian military control through military means, thus effecting a population exchange. In January 1992, Borislav Bogunovic, Deputy Prime Minister of the self-styled Serb Region of Slavonia, Baranja and Western Srem (in Croatia but under Serbian control) announced that 2500 Serb refugees had been resettled in Ilok, a small town in Eastern Slavonia on the right bank of the Danube, over half of whose population, mainly Croats, had fled on 17 October 1991. He said that 4000 more were expected and that the region could settle some 10,000 to 12,000 more Serbs.[231]

By 19 August 1991 some 18,000 Croats and Hungarians had fled Baranja, with 2000 or so Serbs fleeing the same area to the Vojvodina. Estimates in late January 1992 put the population at that time at around 4500 Croats, 6000 Hungarians and 10,000 Serbs, with an influx of some 8000 refugees, mostly Serb women and children, relocated in Baranja from Western Slavonia.[232] The Serbian authorities announced that all those who had left Baranja under pressure since 19 August 1991 (eg. the 20 Croat and Hungarian families reportedly expelled from Batina in Baranja to Hungary by the occupying Chetniks – Serb irregular forces[233]) could return but that this did not apply to those who left 'voluntarily'.[234]

Similarly it was reported that the Croatian authorities were resettling in Istria (Croatia) Croats from Ilok in order to dilute the Italian-speaking population there and possibly bolster support for the ruling Croatian Democratic Community (HDZ) party in an area where they had previously been defeated in elections.[235]

Claims and counter-claims continued. However it does appear that dramatic long term population movements are happening. Of the Serbian refugees from Croatia, large numbers, almost one third, are from areas where there has been no military or para-military activity of note. Specifically 6000 from Zagreb, 2000 from Split, 1000 from Rijeka, while 23,000 Serbs from Sisak (amounting to 90% of the total town population!) are now registered in Serbia according to Radisa Gacic, Federal Minister for Labour, Health Care, Social Policy and Veterans Issues.[236] The Serbian government claims that 60% of Zagreb's Serbs have left in the last one and a half years.[237]

Additionally, in the conflict in Bosnia-Hercegovina, the Serbs have forcibly taken a strip of eastern Bosnia including some predominantly Muslim towns and were attempting to create a corridor under Serb control to link Serbia with the Serb dominated areas of north-western Bosnia and Krajina in Croatia. As a result, thousands of Muslims were reported to have fled the areas.

Serbian forces were reported to have almost totally taken over Goradze in eastern Bosnia where the Muslim population had been inflated by some 20,000 additional Muslim refugees fleeing surrounding areas.[238]

Serbian Radio talked ominously of 'cleansing' the region of Muslims and announced the removal of the Muslim population from Cajnice in south-east Bosnia, claiming that the Muslims were leaving voluntarily. Similar Serbian aggression is expected against the Muslim area of Bihac in north-west Bosnia after Serbian Radio announced that local Serbs were in danger from 'Muslim extremists and fundamentalists'.[239]

While it appears that the number of refugees from Croatia has declined due to the fragile cease- fires and efforts by the EC and UN, the situation remained unstable. There continued to be threat of future serious intercommunal fighting in Kosovo, Macedonia, and the Sandzak. If such hostilities do occur then there are likely to be further massive refugee movements in the area. Serb activities in Slavonia may well presage more dramatic population exchanges. The future remains problematic in the short term and almost certainly for much longer.

Refugees in neighbouring countries

There has been a massive influx of refugees fleeing the hostilities in Yugoslavia – 50,000 between July and mid-December 1991 in addition to those internally displaced within the country. The majority of the refugees went to **Hungary** and of these the largest groups were Croats (90% of the 35,000 who had arrived by late October[240] were in this category), with the remainder being mostly ethnic Hungarians from the Vojvodina.

A committee was formed in Vas county for these refugees with one million *forints* allocated and the Mayor of Horvatzsidan (a town with a majority Croat population on the Hungarian/Austrian border) asked for the settlement to be officially declared a refugee camp.[241] By March 1992 their numbers, which had reached between 40,000 and 50,000 by the end of 1991, had dropped to 25,000, and Hungary expected most of those to stay in Hungary as they had no homes to return to.[242]

The Hungarian Parliament set aside 800m. *forints* to provide for refugees in 1991, with UNHCR contributing $US 2.7m.[243] In November it was announced that the USA planned to give $US 1.8m. and the EC $US 440,000 and that others, including France, Denmark and Germany, would send aid through the ICRC. The UN also expected to collect over $US 3m.[244] The Head of the Refugee Office in the Interior Ministry stated that Hungary had already reached its capacity to provide for refugees in late November 1991, when over 37,000 fleeing Yugoslavians had entered the country.[245]

The Czechoslovak government has raised three million *koruny* for the Czech community in Croatia and has offered to evacuate their children to Czechoslovakia until hostilities cease.[246] In late January 1992 the last of the over 400 ethnic Slovak children who had fled Croatia to Martin in Slovakia in October 1991 returned home. Their temporary stay in Slovakia had been organized with the help of the *Matica Slovenska* cultural organization.[247]

On 2 April the Swiss authorities told Yugoslav refugees to leave the country. Canton authorities said that this applied to some 10,000 people but Swiss TV reported that the real figure was 150,000 to 180,000. The difference may have been due the number of those not registered because of the late introduction of visa requirements by the Swiss for Yugoslavs.[248]

13

EASTERN EUROPE:
POLICIES AND PRACTICE

[CSCE states should]
'extend protection and assistance also to persons with a well-founded
fear of persecution for reasons beyond those defined in the 1951 Geneva
Convention, and to those fleeing war, civil war or other violence, in con-
formity with standards established by current human rights and
humanitarian law norms.'

– Conference on Minorities and Refugees in the CSCE,
Moscow, September 1991.

A recurrent problem in Eastern Europe is the lack of experience in dealing with the new situation of immigrants and transit immigrants. In part this is a lack of administrative and practical skills. But the new situation is even more the result of the rapidity of the changes which have taken place, with economic depression and mass unemployment leading to mass immigration, and of the political fragility of many of the new democracies.

As in many Western European states, there is often great difficulty in resolving the legal status of the growing numbers of immigrants, guest workers and others. For example, in September 1991 the Ministry of the Interior estimated that some 200,000 people were living illegally in Hungary.[249] However, in December 1991 another government spokesperson estimated that the figure was only 40-45,000.[250]

One common factor was that the possible massive influx of people fleeing the disintegrating USSR, which had been forecast at the beginning of 1991, had not occurred by early 1992.

Transient refugees and migrants

In addition to those seeking to remain in Hungary, thousands attempt to cross into Western Europe without authorization. In January 1992

Hungary announced talks with **Austria** and **Czechoslovakia** concerning refoulement of illegal border-crossers, with Hungary seeking guarantees that its neighbours would receive those illegally crossing the border.[251] By early 1992 Hungary had bilateral agreements with Czechoslovakia, **Romania** and the former states of the **USSR** and **Yugoslavia** but these only related to people captured in the immediate border regions.[252]

The agreement with Austria for border violaters from third countries was that they should be sent back to the country of origin, with proceedings started within 72 hours with evidence to show that the person had a legal right to stay in the original country.[253] Most of those fleeing West through Hungary are Romanian citizens, but until recently Hungary could not send Romanians apprehended on the Austrian border back to Romania.

A trilateral expulsion agreement between Hungary, Austria and Romania had, at the time of writing, not yet been signed but was, in effect already operational. Amnesty International has objected to the planned agreement as it did not contain sufficient guarantees to those to be expelled.[254]

Between January and November 1991 Hungary deported over 28,000 border violaters at a cost to the government of over 100m. *forints*.[255] Those expelled included 17,646 from Romania (excluding those caught on the Austrian-Hungarian border), 1602 from Pakistan, 2807 from Turkey, 625 from India, 450 from Ghana, 552 from Bangladesh and 573 Yugoslavs, along with other Africans and Asians.[256] Hungary, Romania and the former USSR have also signed an agreement whereby Hungary is obliged to take back all border violaters leaving Hungary, and other agreements are to be concluded for 'quick transport of those expelled and those taken back'.[257]

In **Czechoslovakia** the main problems relating to groups other than ethnic Czechs or Slovaks are those using Czechoslovakia mainly as a transit route to the West, especially Germany. The majority are from **Romania** and many are Roma (Gypsies). Problems began in mid-1990 when numbers of predominantly ethnic Roma from Romania began to cross Czechoslovakia to the then East Germany but were refused entry. They were housed in camps in North Bohemia in Decin and aid to them was organized by the Czechoslovak Red Cross.

Like other Eastern European states, Czechoslovakia did not possess legislation to cope with this new situation, but (according to unconfirmed information) Romanian citizens in such a position had the right to stay for up to 30 days, guaranteed by a bilateral inter-governmental agreement.[258] By mid-August 1990 almost 3200 had been turned back by East German passport control and were trying to cross into German territory on foot through the woods.[259]

In March 1992 the Czechoslovak Federal Assembly passed a bill on the subject of foreigners to 'protect against an undesirable influx of immigrants'. The bill limited short-term stay but the length of stay could be extended by the Federal Interior Minister. However, it did not apply to those seeking or granted political asylum in the country.[260]

Poland is a major transit point for illegal emigrants to the West, especially to Germany, because of the long shared border. In November 1991 alone, 1013 Romanian citizens, 53 Bulgarians and 27 citizens from the former USSR were caught trying to cross into Germany. Overall this one month saw 1413 citizens from 35 different countries detained trying to leave Poland, mainly to Germany (137 were caught on the southern border with Czechoslovakia and only 12 on Poland's eastern border).[261] The German Federal Frontier protection (BGS) stated that at least 15,406 people tried to enter Germany illegally from Poland in 1991, with almost 6300 turned back. Of the 9110 who succeeded in crossing, 1481 (mostly Europeans) applied for political asylum and the rest were deported.[262]

Large numbers of would-be emigrants to the West via Poland have also been refused entry. The Polish authorities announced that in December 1991, for example, 5533 foreigners, including 4878 former USSR citizens, were denied entry to Poland. The remainder were 206 from Romania, 106 from Mongolia, 76 from Turkey, 51 from Bulgaria and 38 'stateless persons'.[263] In addition, 75 others were expelled from Poland – 57 Romanians, five from Hong Kong, four from Algeria, one from the USA and one from Canada.[264] On the other hand, 186 Poles were deported to Poland in December 1991, including 116 from Germany and 29 from Austria.[265]

While **Bulgaria** has predominantly experienced outward migration, it has recently become a target country for Third World migrants using it as a first stage in their attempted routes to the West. Thousands of such Third World migrants were sleeping rough in the streets of Sofia by mid-1991 – 1800 from Nigeria alone – and the influx was continuing in early 1992.

Reception

In **Hungary** illegal residents from outside Europe are kept at a camp in Kerepestarca which by January 1992 had held some 7000 in all.[266] Inmates are not allowed to leave the camp, and while Hungarian law (which dates from 1982 and is unable to cope with the flood in the

1990s) allows for those facing expulsion to be kept in custody for six days there have been cases of people detained for as long as six months, since the frequent use of forged papers makes it extremely difficult to ascertain true identities and countries of origin.[267] Such circumstances, combined with poor conditions in the camp, led to many disturbances, like the riot of 20 Chinese facing expulsion in late December 1991.[268]

In **Czechoslovakia** the majority of refugees who are not deported as illegal border-crossers are housed in the Czech-lands. In November 1991 the first refugee camp in Slovakia was opened in a former hotel in Adamov-Gbely, Senica district, with five families, including children, from Romania, Yugoslavia and the former USSR.[269]

In **Poland** a Department of Refugees attached to the Interior Ministry was set up in November 1990 which works closely with the PCK and Ministry of Foreign Affairs.[270] The PCK has 11 centres for refugees and in December 1990 there were about 600 people, mostly from Africa (many from Ethiopia), living there.[271] By April 1992 the number was down to 173 refugees who were moved to the residential refugee centre, a former barracks, in Nadarzyn locality, Warsaw Province, set up with help from UNHCR and *Medecins du Monde.*[272]

In February some 30 refugees picketed the Department of Refugees demanding the right to move freely to the West. Some 150 refugees reportedly wanted to leave Poland, their country of first asylum, because of the economic hardships which faced them.[273]

New restrictions

Those Eastern European states which have become targets for asylum-seekers and transient immigrants have partially responded to the influx by new restrictions. These have taken several forms.

On 4 October 1991 restrictions concerning entry to Hungary were introduced and almost 150,000 people, mainly Romanian citizens, were refused entry in the first 30 days alone.[274] Over 20,000 people from 91 countries were expelled from Hungary in 1991 and residence permits were withdrawn from 19,635, with 2103 of these 'freely' choosing to leave the country.[275] In April it was announced that some half a million people had been refused entry since the new restrictions were introduced of whom almost 450,000 were Romanian citizens.[276]

However, it was also announced that the Hungarian Border Guard could not cope with the increased number of organized people-smugglers. According to the Interior Ministry, in the previous two years almost 50,000 people had crossed the border illegally of whom 25,000 had entered with help from people-smugglers.[277]

On 10 January 1992 the Interior Minister, Peter Boross, explained the new conditions for acquiring Hungarian citizenship which effectively applied to 'everybody born of a Hungarian mother'.[278] He stated that, although it was preferable if ethnic Hungarians from the 'so-called annexed territories' (ie. those lost by Hungary in the 1920 Treaty of Trianon, eg. Transylvania) stayed there, it was easy for them to become Hungarian citizens, as had been the case in the 1930s.[279]

The new restrictive climate for 'non-Hungarians' is well illustrated by the Hungarian Director of Public Security at the National Police Command, Major General Dr Andras Turos, who announced new measures to prevent illegal immigrants. He blamed the liberal practices of the previous few years which had allowed 'a flood of people – mostly from Afro-Asian countries' who were 'endangering the security of the country... that nobody can stay there without permission is a question of survival as well as a strict order from the Minister of the Interior'. He also announced reinforcements for border patrols.[280]

While the number of illegal entrants into Hungary had almost doubled for the first three months of 1992 as compared to the first three months of 1991, the number of attempts to leave had declined by 20% showing that more people now view Hungary as a destination country rather than a transit one. The number of Turks has grown noticeably in recent months.[281]

Czechoslovakia initially removed punitive legislation for illegal border-crossing. However, faced with the new situation, the Czechoslovak authorities have introduced tougher measures to deter illegal border-crossers. In December 1991, Law No. 17 was amended so that from 30 December those caught were not merely returned and released but could be imprisoned for up to six months and, in cases of organized action, for up to one year. The penalties for those involved in smuggling people or attempting to bribe officials for the purpose of illegally crossing the borders were raised to five years and eight years for organized large-scale smuggling.[282]

Police announced a total of some 17,800 people caught attempting to cross Czechoslovak frontiers illegally between January and 18 December 1991, of whom 4634 were Romanian citizens, 1878 Vietnamese, 1315 Czechoslovaks and 1050 from Bulgaria.[283]

In late 1990 the Polish government introduced stricter conditions for Romanian citizens entering **Poland** (a minimum of $US 100 when crossing the border even for a stay of less than five days, and at least $US 20 for each succeeding day) but the numbers did not decrease.[284]

Mass repatriation

Both Greece and Italy have resorted to mass repatriation of Albanian citizens. In January and February 1991 an estimated 18,000 Albanians, over half of whom were ethnic Greeks, had fled to **Greece**.[285] Although initially received without apparent hostility, some 1200 were deported back to Albania in the second half of January.[286] Immigrants continued to arrive and the deportations also continued. By 13 February 1991 Greece had handed back over 7100 Albanians.

By the end of 1991, the Greek authorities appeared to have had enough of the thousands of Albanians streaming into the country with little or no means of support and the subsequent rise in crime. Tanjug, the Yugoslav news service, reported on 26 December that there were over 100,000 Albanian citizens in Greece but only a few had valid papers. From May to December 1991, Greece had expelled 81,908 Albanians and Tanjug announced that 800 to 1500 had been turned back at the Greek border in the preceding few weeks.[287]

The Albanian authorities protested at the Greek operation to round up and deport illegal immigrants in an operation known as 'The Broom' (or 'The Sweeper').[288] The Albanian Foreign Minister summoned the Greek Ambassador in Tirana on 14 January 1992 to complain about the 'cruel treatment' of a group of Albanian citizens by Greek soldiers, resulting in two deaths and four seriously injured people being deposited over the border near the Vidohove border crossing.[289]

During a State visit to Albania in May, Greece's Prime Minister, Constantine Mitsotakis, put the number of Albanian refugees in Greece at 150,000, half of whom, he claimed, were there illegally. At a meeting with Albanian President, Sali Berisha, it was agreed to control Albanian emigration to Greece and that Greece should give the right to legal employment to greater numbers of Albanians. The opening of Consulates in Gjirokaster and Ioannina would faciliate granting the necessary visas.[290]

In **Italy**, the International Organization for Migration agreed with the Italian authorities that the best course was for voluntary repatriation, but by mid-1991 only a few Albanians had taken part.[291] By mid-August 1991, the last Albanian migrants in Italy had been deported back to Albania – including military deserters who faced the death penalty if returned. Italy said that it had assurances from the Albanian authorities that these sentences would not be carried out. The refugees claimed that they had been tricked into boarding buses which took them to the airport and then to Tirana after being told that they were going for medical checks before being processed for asylum.[292]

East-West cooperation

In response to the continuing outflow of some of the most productive and educated of its workforce, on 14 June 1991 the Romanian government adopted a decree founding the Romanian Committee for Emigrations[293] and in July it announced that it would support a German plan aimed at stemming the flow of Romanian immigrants and repatriating those already in Germany. Training centres would be established in Romania which would provide land and buildings, while Germany would take responsibility for providing equipment.

The protocol relating to the plan was signed in Bonn on 20 January 1992. The plan has a budget of DM 40m. for over six years. The training in Romania was to include wood-working, construction works, electricity and sanitary installations, and would aim to train up to 1000 workers per year, of whom about half would be Romanian asylum-seekers who had been previously returned from Germany.[294]

In addition, at a conference in Vienna in January 1991, the Romania Project, a mass information scheme to inform Romanians as to the real situation in Western Europe regarding would-be emigrants, was set up with the Swiss authorities agreeing to act as coordinators.[295] While such efforts should be applauded, it remains to be seen how effective they will be in the chaotic internal Romanian context, and how capable they will be of halting the mass emigration.

14

WESTERN EUROPE: TOWARDS COMMON PRACTICE

'The Contracting States shall apply the provisions of this Convention to refugees without discrimination as to race, religion or country of origin.'

– Article 3, UN Convention on Refugees.

Vast discrepancies in law, procedure and traditions have resulted in tremendous inconsistencies in refugee policies and practice throughout Europe. It would be easy to conclude that streamlining is necessary and desirable, but there are complicated issues to be resolved.

Concerned about the imbalances and injustices created by the current situation, the Council of Europe and UNHCR have attempted to tackle the problem. The Council of Europe produced its first Recommendation on Harmonization in 1976 and a second on the Harmonization of National Procedure Related to Asylum in 1981.

The latter does not propose any formal system, but invites European states to check that their procedures and practices meet with standards recommended by the Council of Europe which require: an 'objective and impartial judgement'; referral of the decision to a 'central authority'; 'clear instructions' to immigration officers against refoulement; and permission for the applicant to remain while the asylum request is being examined.[296] The European Consultation on Refugees and Exiles (ECRE) has proposed the creation of a European court to ensure the harmonization of practices and procedures.[297]

In the mid-1980s governments came to the conclusion that they needed to harmonize their asylum policy, but their proposals are not in accordance with the Council of Europe guidelines. On the contrary, the main thrust of their discussions concentrates on measures to reduce the number of asylum-seekers and refugees in Europe at almost any cost.

As individual countries have introduced restrictive measures, refugees have been diverted to those with more open policies. Some states fear that the elimination of internal EC borders proposed for 1992 under the Single European Act may lead to a concentration of refugees in a few states, overburdening their capacity to cope. The main purpose of the harmonization attempts by EC states is therefore likely to be that of uniformly increased restrictions. It is this issue that has been of major concern to NGOs and other humanitarian organizations.

The governments of Western Europe, principally of the EC countries, have come together in order to harmonize their asylum policies, a project which is not devoid of conflicts. States have specific national interests and some groups of countries share common views which are opposed to those of other groups.

A clear north-south cleavage exists on the issue of refugees. Traditionally Spain, Italy, Portugal and Greece are primarily points of entry and transit countries for asylum-seekers who tend to move north to find better conditions of settlement. Moreover Italy, had entered a reservation to its signature of the 1967 Protocol which meant that it did not recognize non-European refugees until 1990. Northern states want their southern neighbours to settle the refugees who arrive on their territories, while the latter are not convinced that they would be able to cope with, or derive any advantage from, this extra burden. This cleavage is reflected in the three fora dealing with harmonization.

Schengen, Trevi and the European Commission

The so-called **Schengen Group**, named after a village in Luxembourg where the first meeting took place on 14 June 1985, brought together the Interior Ministers of five northern countries – Belgium, the Netherlands, Luxembourg, France and Germany. They have met once or twice a year since then to prepare for the elimination of frontier controls on the movement of goods and people between the states involved. They discussed the issues of refugees within the context of immigration control and security and aimed to introduce a single visa area by 1990.

The Schengen Group suspended its work in 1989 as a consequence of events leading to the reunification of Germany, but the agreement nonetheless was signed on 19 June 1990. Italy, which had not been a party to the discussion, joined on 27 November 1990, followed by Spain and Portugal which signed on 25 June 1991. Greece will probably also join.

The Schengen Agreement needs to be ratified by national

Parliaments and a number of laws have to be introduced accordingly in the countries concerned. To date only the French National Assembly has done so, while the Dutch Council of State has raised strong objections to ratification.

The so-called **Trevi Group** was established in 1975 and includes representatives of the Ministries of Interior and of Justice of all 12 EC countries.who meet about every six months to formulate policies on terrorism, drugs and illegal immigration. Conventions emanating from the Trevi Group are under the Council of the Twelve. A sub-group of the Trevi Group's Ad Hoc Group on Immigration was set up in the 1980s, to examine 'the measures to be taken to reach a common policy to put an end to the abusive use of the right of asylum'.

The 12 states have moved fast in drafting two conventions. The Convention Determining the State Responsible for Examining Applications for Asylum Lodged in One of the Member States of the European Community (thereafter called the **Dublin Convention** in this text) was signed in Dublin on 15 June 1990 by all EC members with the exception of Denmark which signed it in June 1991.

The second convention relates to controls at EC external borders. It defines what constitutes a point of entry, and how to deal with agreements with third states (non-EC members) and small border traffic. It includes a proposal to draw up a computerized list of *persona non grata* on EC territory. Another of its significant concerns is the harmonization of policies and practices of EC states on the question of visas, with the possibility of issuing Community visas.

The signature of the Convention planned for the Rome meeting in December 1991 (in this book hereafter referred to as the **Rome Convention**) was postponed as a result of disagreements over Gibraltar. The two conventions are subject to ratification by member states' Parliaments after being signed by all the 12 states.

A committee consisting of one official representative of the government of each member state will examine questions concerning the application and interpretation of each convention. Two additional documents are being considered which may result in further international agreements: a draft convention on the transfer of proceedings in criminal matters and a summary document on the strengthening of police cooperation.

The **European Commission** makes proposals for directives and regulations which constitute Community law and implements Community decisions. Its sub-group on asylum (part of the Ad Hoc Group on Immigration, not to be confused with the other group on Immigration of the Council of the Twelve group) consists of senior civil servants who prepared a document on asylum within the broad implementation of the Single European Act. This was not concerned with 'the harmonization of the law of asylum in general but only of those provisions and practices vital for the removal of frontier control'.[298]

However, governments have not accepted that the Commission has any competence on the question of asylum, mainly because the member states are concerned about infringements of sovereignty. The Commission's *Avant-Projet de Directive* (Draft Proposal for a Council Directive) appeared to be shelved but may have influenced the Trevi discussion. The Commission's role might take on a renewed significance, however, as a result of the progress of political union within the Community.

It is important to consider the main items on which the discussions on harmonization have focused.

Requests for asylum

One of the main purposes of harmonization has been to introduce some order into the handling of asylum applications. With the aim of avoiding multiple applications the parties concerned soon established the principle that each application should be examined by one single state. The most difficult task then became drawing up guidelines to determine which state was responsible.

The possibility of giving the applicant the choice of country was rejected on the grounds that asylum-seekers, unlike immigrants, are not supposed to plan their emigration but go wherever possible.[299] (Ensuring that refugees do not congregate in the more prosperous states with higher standards of living is likely to have been the real reason for this decision.)

Governments retain as a guideline the notion of 'country of first asylum'. To define beyond doubt what this meant, the elucidation put forward was that: 'the more one state manifested its agreement to the arrival or even to the stay of an asylum-seeker, the more this state became responsible'.[300]

Granting a visa was deemed to be the most crucial indicator. The three bodies studied, the Schengen Group, the Council of the Twelve (Dublin Convention) and the European Commission, expressed similar opinions on this. The proposed rules are summarized as follows:

The main **criterion** is which state authorized entry (Schengen Agreement Art. 30, Dublin Convention Art. 5). The state which granted a residence permit or the visa of 'longest duration' was to be deemed responsible. If a state did not require a visa it was nonetheless deemed responsible as this constituted an 'implicit agreement' to the arrival of the asylum-seeker. When a visa was valid in several countries, as is already the case in Benelux, the country responsible would be the one where the asylum application was handed in. If an asylum-seeker was found in an irregular situation the first border reached would determine which state was responsible.

In addition, the Schengen Group stated that they aimed to achieve a 'uniform visa area'. In this eventuality (as pointed out by the Netherlands) most of the detailed clauses mentioned above would become void and two criteria would remain: the country where the application was handed in (if the asylum-seeker's situation was regular) and the border reached first (in an irregular situation).[301]

The Schengen Group, the Council of the Twelve and the European Commission all broached the issue of expulsion in order to reinforce the question of responsibility. To this end the proposal stipulates that each state must ensure the expulsion of applicants to whom it has refused asylum in order to prevent them from drifting into neighbouring countries. Moreover, to protect each country from the 'irresponsibility' of others, a 'readmission clause' was included in the proposals. Consequently, the country in charge of examining the application will have to take back asylum-seekers who may have entered other member countries irregularly (Schengen Agreement Art. 33, Dublin Convention Art. 10). But the readmission clause would remain void if the relevant state had expelled the unsuccessful applicant (Schengen Agreement Art. 34, Dublin Convention Art. 10).

The general tone of these proposals seems to indicate that states are reluctant to settle refugees. Their one redeeming feature from the refugees' point of view is that such agreements may reduce the risk of remaining 'in orbit', pushed on from country to country. However, as was pointed out by the Dutch Council of State[302] it may have precisely the opposite effect, of increasing the numbers of refugees in orbit as each state may argue that it is not responsible for examining the asylum request.

The Council of the Twelve and the Commission introduced an additional criterion to determine the state responsible for examining asylum requests, that of close family links; and a transfer of responsibility is planned if need be.[303] The Schengen Group also added that the treaty-making state that had granted refugee status and residence to an alien should be bound to take into consideration an asylum application from a member of his family if all the parties concerned agree to it. In this instance, the definition of member of his family is deemed to include spouse, unmarried minor children (under 18 years of age), and father and mother of unmarried minors. Although Belgium and the Netherlands had expressed reservations about this definition,[304] it was incorporated into the final text of the agreement.[305]

These two bodies also made it possible for a state other than the one deemed responsible to examine the request in accordance with its national procedure if it had special ties with the applicant or 'for humanitarian reasons, based in particular on family or cultural grounds' (Dublin Convention Art. 9). Within the Schengen Group it was agreed that asylum requests could be examined by a state which was not responsible 'for special reasons concerning national law'.[306]

The Schengen Group also considered an incentive to ensure strict application of the agreements: it launched the idea of creating a common fund designated to cover the costs of deporting 'illegals'. However, its terms were not decided as reservations were expressed by France and Germany[307] and it does not appear in the definitive text.

In a further attempt to control the arrival of asylum-seekers the Schengen Group discussed the possibility of imposing sanctions on transport companies carrying foreigners with irregular documents. This suggestion was not taken up immediately, as French officials expressed reluctance to hand over the checking of documents to airline employees who might not be French nationals. It is worth noting that Air France and the SNCF (French national railways) have already been fined heavily and have refused to pay such fines.

However, the Schengen states finally agreed on tackling transporters. The Schengen Agreement imposes on air-, sea- and land-transporters the obligation of taking back immediately an alien refused entry; they must also take measures to ensure that aliens have the required documents to travel. In order to enforce this, the Schengen states will be committed to introducing sanctions accordingly.[308] They will also introduce penal sanctions on anyone who 'for purposes of gain' helps or tries to help an alien enter the territory without the required documents.[309] The Dublin and Rome Conventions also impose sanctions on transporters (Rome Convention Art. 14).

Procedures

Procedures have not given rise to a great deal of debate, as a consensus was rapidly reached. The three bodies agreed that national procedures should be left as they stood to handle applications.[310] The Council of the Twelve and the Schengen Group do not accept any departure from this model.

As for the Commission, it put forward the creation of a central EC-wide consultative committee[311] to ensure that decisions taken in one state did not contradict the statute law of another. In the Commission's opinion, this is the only way to secure the respect of 'Community standards' and the enforceability of negative decisions in all the member states.

The Commission's directive adds that this consultative committee does not constitute yet another echelon in the procedure and solely imparts advice which is not legally binding but which should be taken into account because of its 'moral strength'. Despite the Commission's concern to demonstrate that such a committee would in no way encroach on national sovereignty, the member states have expressed their disapproval of this proposal.

Finally the Commission is the only body to have proposed the creation of an 'abridged procedure'.[312] The Commission argues that several states already have one and that it could be generalized and streamlined to help decrease the overload of applications. Such a procedure is designed to deal with three situations: successive or simultaneous applications, an application whose responsibility rests with a non-EC country, and a 'manifestly unfounded application'.

Exchange of information

All three bodies make mention of an exchange of information on asylum-seekers. The Commission proposed to exchange general information. The Council of the Twelve is already circulating statistics. The Schengen Group and the Dublin Convention prepared a detailed list of the type of information to be gathered, including general information on national procedures, statistical data on the monthly arrival of asylum-seekers and their breakdown by nationality, the emergence or significant increase of certain groups and more specific information on the countries of origin (Dublin Convention Art. 14) and on individual asylum-seekers; this also includes information on members of the family,[313] their documents, itineraries, and decisions taken about their cases. For this purpose the Schengen Information System (SIS) will be computerized.

Details regarding the motives for the asylum application and the decision comprise the only information which would be subject to the applicant's consent.[314] French reservations did not preclude an agreement on this point.[315] Moreover, the Rome Convention proposes to circulate a computerized list of *persona non grata* on EC territory.

From the point of view of the asylum-seekers, information concerning their countries of origin alone might be beneficial if it was suffi-ciently accurate. All the other registers of data mentioned above belong to a vast police operation which appears necessary only if asy-lum-seekers are considered *a priori* unwelcome and a threat to European states.

Circulation of foreigners

A broad discrepancy exists between the views of the Council of the Twelve (Rome Convention) and the Commission on the one hand and the Schengen states on the other concerning the circulation of asylum-seekers and refugees within the confines of the EC.

The Schengen proposal treats refugees in the same way as other aliens holding a residence permit from one of the contracting states. They will be able to move freely within the borders of the Schengen states if they have a valid travel document, but will be obliged to declare themselves to the competent authorities on entry or within three days of entry (at the choice of the contracting parties).[316] Some asylum-seekers might be included in this provision if they hold a pro-visional residence permit and a travel document issued by one of the Schengen states.[317] In April 1988, the French had raised objections to this proposal on account of the heavy workload that would be involved 'with little effect',[318] but they dropped them thereafter.

The Rome Convention and the Commission adopt a different atti-tude, arguing that the absence of border checks will make it impossible to prevent asylum-seekers and refugees from circulating and they con-clude that it is best to try and put some order into their movements. According to the Commission Directive and the Rome Convention, refugees should be allowed to stay in another EC state for up to three months without a visa,[319] and asylum-seekers who cross an internal border must register with the police within 72 hours. The Directive stipulates that they are allowed to stay up to a month but cannot call upon health and social benefits.

This last point will probably have to be modified as it contravenes the established rules on the rights to benefits granted by the Social Affairs Directorate.[320] The Rome Convention on controls at EC external borders, still to be signed by the member states, proposed to allow any alien holding a residence permit from one of the EC states to travel freely 'for a short stay' within EC borders (if the residence permit still has more than four months to run).[321]

All the documents constituting the basis for these agreements were been kept confidential while they were discussed internally as well as details of the meetings of the Schengen Group and the Council of the Twelve which remain shrouded in secrecy. Observers from NGOs or UNHCR were not permitted. The Commission was allowed to send an observer to the Council of the Twelve; the European Parliament also requested permission to attend, thus far without success. The Commission has sent its directive to UNHCR and to independent experts from many European governments for comments.

15

WESTERN EUROPE: CRITICISMS OF THE NEW ARRANGEMENTS

'In order that people at risk may be afforded effective protection, Amnesty International seeks to ensure that refugee-determination procedures and the procedures followed at airports and borders are adequate to identify asylum-seekers who would be at risk of human rights violations if sent against their will to the countries they have fled or to a third country. It calls on all states to ensure their procedures include certain minimum safeguards which are essential in helping to identify and ensure the protection of such people.'

– Amnesty International Report 1991.

The new conventions have been drawn up under international law and not European Community law. The effect of this is that they are not subject to the jurisdiction of the European Court in Luxembourg, and they can be developed in secrecy and are not subject to public debate. Leaks about the negotiations have provoked widespread protest including a joint press conference of NGO's and MEPs in June 1988, a petition handed in to the Schengen states and numerous individual meetings and discussions. In April 1989, the *Commission de Sauvegarde du Droit d'Asile* (CSDA), a French NGO network, submitted a manifesto supported by 126 agencies to Mr Emile Casimajou, the inter-ministerial delegate for the Schengen Agreements.

In April 1990 Amnesty International published a pamphlet criticizing the new initiatives entitled *Harmonization of Asylum Policy in Europe: Amnesty International's Concerns*. In the same month a report was produced by the Permanent Committee of Experts on International Alien, Refugee and Criminal Law Policy[322] which stresses that 'between democracies such secrecy falls short of all acceptable standards'. *France Terre D'Asile* (FTDA) campaigned against the signing of the Dublin Convention and a petition of about 200 signatures was sent to the Council of Europe and to Members of the European Parliament.[323] In Germany, Caritas, an international NGO, held a meeting on the Dublin Convention in January 1991.

A variety of other organizations and institutions have added their voices to the criticism.

UNHCR, which has been almost totally excluded from the discussions, has produced several documents relating to refugees in Europe.

The **Council of Europe**, comprising 26 European countries, has two main organs. The Committee of Ministers may make recommendations giving general guidelines on policies or approve conventions and agreements on standards and procedures which, to be binding on a state, have to be signed and ratified; within this body the relevant committee for refugee matters is the Committee on Migration with its expert group, the Ad Hoc Committee of Experts on the Legal Aspects of Refugees (Comité Ad Hoc sur les Asilés et les Réfugiés – CAHAR). Its views tend to be closer to governmental views than do those of other Council of Europe Committees.

The Council of Europe Parliamentary Assembly is composed of members appointed from each of the member states' Parliament and it makes recommendations to the Committee of Ministers. Two of the Assembly's committees are directly involved in the matter of refugees: the Parliamentary Committee on Refugees, Migration and Demography and the Resettlement Fund Committee. They have produced reports and recommendations which are very sympathetic to refugees. NGOs with consultative status can participate in this work.

The **European Parliament** with its 518 elected members is mostly an advisory body. It has put refugees on the agenda in several of its committees, notably the Political Affairs Committee and the Committee on Legal Affairs and Citizens' Rights.

Finally, humanitarian and human rights NGOs as well as refugee agencies, most of which take part in the **European Consultation on Refugees and Exiles** (ECRE) founded in 1975, have been closely involved in monitoring policies and making proposals for amendments and improvements at national and international levels.

The core of the objections to the process of harmonization has been in the restrictive tendencies expressed in these projects and the restrictive practices already implemented by most countries. All the bodies mentioned above have objected to the secrecy which has characterized the governmental discussions on these agreements. The European Parliament in particular has protested at having no say in the matter. Secrecy has precluded public debate on decisions which involve important civil liberties issues, and has not allowed for consultation.

However, a recent change of attitude is to be noted among both the Schengen Group and the Ad Hoc Group on Immigration of the Twelve which demonstrates a greater openness. UNHCR welcomes the recognition in the Schengen Agreement (Art. 28) of the value of cooperation and coordination with UNHCR and is preparing recommendations regarding the implementation of the Agreement.[324]

The Ad Hoc Group has invited the European Commission to collaborate; it has also held meetings with UNHCR and even with NGOs. ECRE attended a first meeting on 16 May 1990 in Brussels, too late to attempt to influence the drafting of the Dublin Convention; but it forwarded suggestions regarding the Rome Convention.[325]

Schengen, Dublin and Rome

Comments made by organizations critical of the Schengen, Dublin and Rome agreements include a number of positive points. All welcome in the Schengen and Dublin documents the recognition of the 1951 Geneva Convention without geographical limitation, which had been absent from earlier drafts. UNHCR commends the cooperation between states introducing the question of responsibility for asylum claims and the readmission clauses ensuring that states fulfil their obligations to process asylum applications;[326] this should help towards tackling the problem of 'refugees in orbit' and is consistent with earlier recommendations of UNHCR.[327]

UNHCR also appreciates the inclusion of provisions allowing states the flexibility to admit family members and other persons on humanitarian grounds; it particularly promotes a generous implementation of these provisions to include consideration of language, education and former association (which are stipulated in the Dublin Convention). The sharing of information on refugee trends and countries of origin is also seen as a useful contribution.

Finally, those who are in favour of European integration interpret the elaboration of these agreements as a constructive move testifying to the political commitment of the EC member states.[328] Eagerness to further this aim could very well explain why France dropped most of the objections it had raised during the elaboration of the Schengen text.

However, the numerous criticisms levelled against them means the balance sheet still tilts against Schengen and the other Conventions.

In the first place doubts are raised about the actual efficiency of implementing the rules determining the state responsible for processing an asylum claim. Moreover, the criteria determining the state responsible do not take into account UNHCR recommendations on the asylum-seeker's intention.[329] It is also pointed out that it will remain difficult to identify the first country of arrival when the person has entered Europe illegally.[330]

As noted in Chapter 14, the Dutch Council of State had already warned that the number of refugees in orbit might be increased rather than decreased by these arrangements, the transfer procedure possibly causing long delays. As far as the Netherlands are concerned transfer of responsibility is simply not allowed by their municipal law and according to the Council of State would be tantamount to a breach of the Geneva Convention.[331]

The discrepancy between different states' procedures and criteria in interpreting the Geneva Convention renders the whole process unfair and may lead to unredeemable refoulements, since the decision of the state responsible is binding on all the others. Individual claims could be rejected in one state which might have been accepted or recognized in another.[332] Heightened pressure for more restrictive measures in the states adopting more liberal criteria might also ensue. It might even lead directly to a lowering of social rights standards as illustrated by the measures proposed by Denmark before it signed the Dublin Convention.[333] These measures could therefore contravene the prohibition of discrimination (Geneva Convention, Art.3).

The exchange of information incorporated in the three agreements/conventions caused great concern as regards the data on individual asylum-seekers. Guarantees about the confidentiality of the data appear to be insufficient. Even the Dublin Convention which pledges to respect the European Convention for the Protection of Individuals with regard to Automatic Processing of Personal Data (Art. 15 Section 12) is open to criticism.[334] Indeed, some EC states are not party to this convention which has been signed only by France, the UK, Luxembourg, the Federal Republic of Germany, Spain and Denmark; and, in addition, in some countries, such as the Netherlands, the police are exempt from respecting the Convention. Furthermore, there is no restriction on the exchange of data. Such loopholes are all the more significant, since the very life and safety of the individuals concerned are at stake.

In the case of the Schengen agreement, the regulations governing the circulation of refugees will constitute a deterioration on previous conditions: the Strasbourg Convention, today signed by all EC states except France, allows the freedom of movement of Convention refugees (but not of settlement), whereas the Schengen agreement, while not requesting a visa, requires that refugees 'declare themselves' to the competent authorities. Emphasis on post-entry controls general-ly raises preoccupations about the victimization of people who do not 'look' European, a point which applies to large numbers of refugees and asylum-seekers.[335]

Sanctions against transporters, combined with visas, have perhaps attracted the most severe criticisms and are considered in the next chapter. As for sanctions against smugglers and traffickers, they call for a more precise definition to ensure that the work of humanitarian organizations is not affected. It is feared that the interpretation of 'family' will remain narrow, thus affecting unmarried couples, Islamic marriages, marriages that cannot be proven if documents have gone missing, persons who cannot divorce (like many Latin Americans) but who live with another partner.[336]

The Executive Committee's powers are regarded undemocratic since it is not subject to control or supervision, either by national Parliaments or by the Luxembourg Court of Justice.[337]

In the three documents concerned no mention is made of persons who do not fall under the Geneva Convention but who might be in need of protection (such as victims of torture or generalized violence). The European Convention on Human Rights and the Convention for the Prevention of Torture, which are important instruments in defin-ing those in need of protection, are not mentioned in the agreements. This is not a negligible omission, as all the refugee organizations have pointed out, since it affects thousands of people.

The relationship between the Schengen agreement and Rome and Dublin Conventions and their consequences for EC development are an issue on which many questions remain unanswered. Is the Schengen agreement supposed to be temporary until a larger agree-ment is achieved or is it to provide an alternative to the conventions of the 12 by absorbing more and more members?[338] Where Schengen and Dublin/Rome differ (as on provisions regulating the circulation of refugees and asylum-seekers), which will prevail?

In any event, the Schengen agreement seems to have helped to speed up the work of the Ad Hoc Group on Immigration, since these conventions focus attention on the refugee issue. Sweden (1 July 1991) and Austria (31 July 1991) have already applied to join the EC and Switzerland is said to be very keen to join the Dublin Convention. However accession is only open to EC member states. Some of the Central and Eastern European countries are also reported to be con-templating joining the EC. In the meantime bilateral agreements have been signed (between the Schengen group and Poland) and others are in the offing (with Hungary and Czechoslovakia). As a consequence, the Council of Europe has expressed its concern that these conventions may lead to overburdening states which are not party to them with increased requests for asylum.[339]

The development from 1985 of European initiatives leading to the Schengen, Dublin and Rome agreements has prompted additional or alternative possible scenarios for asylum-seekers and refugees in Europe. UNHCR, a conference of NGOs in The Hague and the Standing Committee of Experts on International Immigration Refugee and Criminal Law have produced such outline plans.

Concerning the Schengen agreement, an additional protocol or a joint declaration is deemed necessary for further safeguards and fair implementation.[340] The need to act within the structure of the EC and within EC law is emphasized. UNHCR proposed a European Commission on Asylum and Refugees,[341] including representatives from the EC member states, the European Commission and UNHCR, with a judge from the Luxembourg Court of Justice as president. Its functions would include making assessments of the situation in countries of origin and interpreting the legal provisions of international and Community law.

According to the Standing Committee, a Court of Justice should be designated (following on from the example of Article 177 of the Treaty of Rome), which would hand down rulings on matters relating to the Schengen regulations referred to it by the national courts. The Hague NGO conference recommended the creation of a high-level EC Advisory Committee on Human Rights to advise the institutions of the European Community and a consultative committee composed of representatives of European governments, UNHCR, other inter-governmental organizations and NGOs.

The European Convention on Human Rights is put forward as one of the main legal instruments to be taken into account when dealing with asylum-seekers and refugees in Europe. It is proposed that a protocol to it should be adopted by European states, covering the right of individuals to seek and be granted asylum, and to have access to a fair and efficient procedure for the determination of refugee status and the examination of the asylum claim, as well as procedural standards.[342]

On the question of procedures, UNHCR made concrete and precise recommendations concerning the accelerated procedure for manifestly unfounded cases and a shortened procedure in the case of mass influx situations, together with plans for a pooling of officers seconded from other countries to the crisis area. But before the implementation of an accelerated procedure, the NGOs and the Council of Europe are unanimous about the need to harmonize procedures and criteria.

Additional concerns

In addition to specific criticisms of the Schengen, Dublin and Rome documents, other concerns have been voiced by humanitarian and human rights organizations dealing with refugees, in particular that refugees have been increasingly considered as ordinary aliens or migrant workers.[343]

The growing tendency to handle first interviews on asylum at airports or ports of entry has meant that untrained immigration officers have to deal with these cases. This has prompted the Council of Europe to discuss a recommendation for the development of training programmes for officials in charge of training border officers and also those involved in refugee status determination.[344]

The Council of Europe's Parliamentary Assembly also made other recommendations: an agreement on the harmonization of policies on the reception of asylum-seekers, particularly at airports, to be prepared before January 1993; a European code, to be distributed widely in asylum-seekers'countries of origin and upon arrival, on their rights and the relevant procedures; and sufficient suitable accommodation and human treatment to be secured.[345] Amnesty International has also protested against the procedure at borders.

UNHCR, the European Parliament and the Council of Europe have all objected to the restrictive interpretation of the concept of a refugee and the increased standard of proof requested of the applicant,[346] while ECRE has analyzed in detail the varying interpretations in European countries.[347]

Refoulement has become such an object of concern that ECRE has developed guidelines indicating which safeguards have to be respected before any asylum-seeker is expelled on any grounds, including claims deemed to be 'manifestly unfounded' or those supposed to have been in a 'country of first asylum'.

According to these guidelines a country to which a state proposes to send back an asylum-seeker should ensure a basic protection, including protection against refoulement, plus effective access to a local procedure and efficient and adequate resettlement facilities and facilities for voluntary repatriation.[348] The document makes special mention of countries of first arrival, to which applicants had been returned but had then found themselves back in their country of origin from which they had fled. The concept of 'safe country' used by Denmark on which these actions are based is misleading. A country may be 'safe' in so far as it will not persecute the asylum-seeker but very 'unsafe' if it returns the person to a country where he or she fears persecution.

An issue of equal concern to governments and other bodies is the length of procedures which has created a backlog of pending cases in most European countries. UNHCR has been working on this issue in its consultations with governments which appear to retain the notion of summary procedures for manifestly unfounded cases, and the practice of a full oral hearing at the start of the procedure.[349] An appeal procedure is not always available in the event of a negative decision nor does it always have a suspensive effect on refoulement as has been the case in the UK.

Non-Convention refugees have not been an issue in any of the governmental negotiations on harmonization. Their existence is not even acknowledged, so much so that UNHCR found it necessary to remind the EC Commission to include them in its Directive.[350] But this category of refugees ranks high on the agenda of non-governmental bodies.[351]

A new and puzzling phenomenon is developing in the area of refugees in Europe and which is likely to draw greater attention: the arrival of an increasing number of unaccompanied minors.[352] It has grown to such proportions that UNHCR has prepared a special report and International Social Service produced a brochure on the question.

An implicit assumption is made throughout government negotiations, including asylum issues under police and security measures: that refugees, terrorists and drug traffickers fall into the same category. Muslim asylum-seekers are doubly affected by these prejudices. It almost appears as though Europe was fortifying the boundaries of Christendom against all alien elements.

All the organizations mentioned in this chapter differ from governments in their general approach to the question. They adopt a global view on the question of refugees in Europe, and NGOs in particular stress the responsibilities of Europe in finding solutions to the world refugee crisis. Both the European Parliament and the Council of Europe[353] have promoted a developmental approach to refugee issues and propose to link respect for human rights with assistance for social and economic development.

ECRE has put on the agenda the question of 'internal refugees' or internally displaced people who cannot benefit from international protection or assistance. The plight of the Kurds in Iraq in the wake of the Gulf War illustrated the necessity for the international community not to remain indifferent to such situations.

Finally, a question which has not been addressed in the discussion of harmonization has been the resettlement policies which many of the non-governmental bodies follow. These constantly press for an improvement of settlement conditions and particularly emphasize the predicament in which asylum-seekers and non-Convention refugees find themselves as a result of the severe limitations on their social and economic rights. Moreover, UNHCR stresses the interdependent relationship between the uneven distribution of refugees and asylum-seekers in Europe and the discrepancies in socio-economic conditions offered to them across Europe.

16

WESTERN EUROPE:
THE POLITICAL BACKLASH

1. The Contracting States shall not expel a refugee lawfully in their ter-
ritory save on grounds of national security or public order.
2. The expulsion of such a refugee shall only be in pursuance of a deci-
sion reached in accordance with due process of law. Except where com-
pelling reasons of national security otherwise require, the refugee shall
be allowed to submit evidence to clear himself, and to appeal to and be
represented for the purpose before competent authority or a person or
persons specially designated by the competent authority.
3. The Contracting States shall allow a refugee a reasonable period
within which to seek legal admission to another country.'

– Article 32, UN Convention on Refugees.

In the late 1980s and into the 1990s, a qualitative change has taken
place on the part of governments, the media and the general public concerning the general perception of asylum-seekers and
refugees. In many ways that perception has assumed a fantasy life
of its own out of all proportion with the reality. A complex inter-rela-
tion of reactions fuels the attitudes displayed by governments, the
media and the general public.

Governments

Governments, and political figures whether in government or opposi-
tion, display considerable disarray when faced with the arrival of asylum-seekers. More and more stringent laws are passed, declarations
against 'bogus' refugees outbid one another, effectively incriminating
both refugees and immigrants.

Firstly, European governments are disturbed by the fact that the
numbers of asylum-seekers are neither predictable nor controllable in
principle since their acceptance is conditioned by an international

convention which by its very nature does not accept the notion of a numerical limit. Their entitlement to protection is limited only by the genuineness of their claim.

Secondly, governments do not appear to know how to distinguish those who have a valid claim from others. Perhaps they like to believe that many asylum-seekers are 'false', thereby conjuring away the need to accept more than a small proportion of the total. Finally, many governments have yielded to certain strands of public opinion which favour control over all immigration, particularly in times of recession. In this conjuncture no distinction is made between immigrants and refugees. Moreover, many politicians endeavour to enhance their popularity by pandering to their electorate at the expense of both.

In addition, a number of extraordinary measures have recently been taken in various European countries concerning asylum-seekers and refugees. In the UK, the Home Secretary took two controversial decisions in the last two months of 1991 which led to demands for his resignation. He ordered the deportation of a Zairian asylum-seeker back to Zaire, despite a court order not to do so, and also of a Sikh separatist to India. In France a Moroccan refugee, Abdelmoumen Diouri, was deported to Gabon on 20 June 1991 and the Paris administrative tribunal ordered the reversal of this decision on 10 July. In Norway, the chief of security police, Mr Urdal, was obliged to resign after allowing Mossad agents to interrogate ten Palestinian asylum-seekers.[354] In Belgium, Zaventem airport transit lounge was, for a time, transformed into a prison complete with barbed wire, dog patrols, and spotlights at night on curtainless windows.[355] Communes (the municipal authorities in Belgium) are regularly falling foul of the law by refusing to register refugees, thus leaving them homeless and deprived of health care and education for their children, as was the case in Namur and Huy in October 1991.[356]

Media

The media generally exacerbate the situation. Restrictive measures and declarations in turn enhance hostility and prejudice against foreigners and refugees, and these hostile attitudes appear to be given some justification when political leaders confirm them, or fail to condemn them. Thus the circle continues, spinning into greater hatred and prejudice.

A few examples from the many available will illustrate this process. In the UK the preliminary period prior to the passing of a new and very strict Asylum Bill was marked by several declarations by the Prime Minister, John Major, embracing both refugees and immigrants: 'We must not be wide open to all [new] comers just because Rome, Paris and London are more attractive than Bombay or Algiers',[357] a statement he repeated at the Conservative Party conference in October 1991. Some sections of the press reported such statements in an inflammatory manner.

In France Jean-Marie Le Pen, leader of the racist *Front National*, seems to set the tone for the debate on immigration and several leaders of other parties have followed suit. Jacques Chirac of the Gaullist RPR declared 'il y a overdose' in a speech about immigrants and spoke against family reunion, evoking:

> *'an overcrowded family with the father, three or four wives and 20 or so kids, who receives 50,000 Francs in social security payments, obviously without working... not to mention the noise and the smell...'*[358]

Giscard d'Estaing of the UDF quoted the abuse of asylum applications and the arrival of Albanians in Italy to claim that:

> *'the type of problem we will have to face is moving from that of immigration...and verges on invasion'*

and promotes the return to *jus sanguinis* in France.[359]

As for Le Pen, he plainly warned of 'the likely invasion of our territory by foreign hordes' which would justify 'recourse to armed forces' in a meeting of the Right Wing Group of the European Parliament in London.[360]

The Public

The backlash from governments has been matched and, in some cases, superseded by that of the public. In several European countries refugees and asylum-seekers were the victims of violent physical attacks. In Sweden during the spring and summer of 1990 there were several attacks on reception centres with Molotov cocktails in which one was burnt to the ground;[361] in October 1991 one bomb attack was aimed at a reception centre in Göteborg and another destroyed the home of a Vietnamese family in Oskarshram. In Germany, according to the Federal Bureau for Crime Prevention, 904 criminal offences were committed in October against foreigners including asylum-seekers.[362] The German ombudsman for foreigners resigned on 12 September 1991 in protest at a lack of government support in fighting an 'alarming xenophobia'.[363]

In the UK about 7000 racist attacks are reported every year, which represents only a small percentage of the real figures.[364] In Switzerland in 1991 refugee hostels were assaulted in Interlaken and in Thun, and in the Basle region[365] the Federal Public Prosecutor's Office has counted 25 violent or suspicious incidents involving refuges for refugees. Again in Switzerland certain municipalities have stopped paying their membership fee to the Red Cross and some individual donors are refusing to support Caritas and Protestant Inter-Aid, arguing that too many resources are devoted to refugees.[366] In France opinion polls organized by SOFRES, a polling agency, reveal increasing support for the *Front National*'s racist anti-immigration policies.[367]

All these incidents are indicative of the general atmosphere regarding asylum-seekers and refugees in Western Europe. The European Parliament set up two working parties to prepare reports on racism and xenophobia, and expressed great alarm about the deterioration registered between the first report in 1984 and the second in October 1990. This led to a solemn common declaration against racism and xenophobia signed by all the EC member states and the three main EC institutions: the Council of Ministers, the Commission and the European Parliament.[368]

A less favourable attitude to refugees is also expressed through the passing of new laws in several European countries. The Danish Minister of Justice is proposing to remove de facto refugees' right to remain in Denmark and to decrease social benefits granted to refugees in order to make Denmark less attractive to potential refugees, in preparation for the signature of the Dublin Convention.[369] The Dutch government's proposal for the Aliens Act, which will make it possible to detain certain categories of asylum-seekers, has been agreed in Parliament.[370]

The revised Swiss asylum law allows the Federal Council to draw up a list of countries where persecution of any sort is deemed not to exist; it can then decide not to consider applications for refugee status from any of their nationals. The decision takes immediate effect and no appeal is permissible.[371] The list to date includes Czechoslovakia, Hungary, Poland, Bulgaria, Algeria and India. In Sweden there are plans to abolish the current provisions for de facto refugees and conscientious objectors.[372]

In the UK a whole package is being prepared, including an Asylum Bill, draft immigration rules and draft asylum appeals rules. These will introduce fingerprinting for asylum-seekers, extend the provisions of the Carriers Liability Act to transit passengers and increase the fine, allow for extended powers of detention and reduce asylum-seekers' right to council housing. Among factors which may lead to a refusal of refugee status are the destruction of documents, the involvement in 'any activities' in the UK 'calculated to enhance his claim to refugee status' (ie. protesting against the regime which persecuted him or her), and the supposed opportunity an applicant may have had to move to a safer part of the country in which he or she feared persecution. Applications for leave of appeal will have to be made within two days of the asylum-seekers' receiving notice of a negative decision, with the assumption that the person has received it the day after it has been posted. The passing of the law was postponed on account of the general election in April 1992 but is to be introduced in the new Parliament.

Moreover, a number of other trends are appearing or being confirmed in the drafting or implementation of policies and procedures. Some of these had earlier been tried in some European countries and were taken up by the harmonization process, the Schengen Agreement, the Trevi Group and the relevant conventions. As a consequence, while they are now being adopted throughout the signatory states, they also influence others.

Key issues

Airline sanctions
Penalties against airlines have now become current practice in several European countries and will soon be implemented in all EC member states under the Schengen Agreement and the Dublin and Rome Conventions.

As yet, it has not been proven whether such sanctions have resulted in a reduction in the number of asylum-seekers in the countries concerned, but they certainly have led airlines to take a number of measures to control their passengers, 'ranging from the legal, such as the introduction of staff training courses and the use of more sophisticated equipment to detect forgeries, to the illegal, such as unauthorized deportations'.[373]

Governments constantly claim that these measures are not directed at genuine refugees but at economic migrants trying to circumvent immigration rules. However, sanctions against transporters, combined with the general use of visas imposed on citizens of non-European countries, seem to affect genuine refugees more than any other group.

There is no doubt that it can be problematic, and frequently dangerous, for a person who is being persecuted or targeted by a state to obtain a valid passport from that state and then attempt to obtain a visa from a foreign consulate, thereby drawing attention to his or her intention to escape.[374]

These sanctions have already entailed numerous interventions by airline staff. In 1989, three Kurdish asylum-seekers were prevented from leaving the plane at London's Heathrow airport by airline staff. This resulted in their being returned to Turkey where they were severely tortured (including electric shocks to the genitals) for 34 days. In August 1991 airline staff did not allow the wife of a Somalian refugee in Denmark to board the plane because they 'thought' that her Danish visa was forged.[375] The Scandinavian Airline System has drawn up a list of observations which helps to spot potential asylum-seekers (ie. when the person has a one-way ticket, does not speak English or looks or seems to be poor) and advises its staff to act in the interest of the company and refuse the passenger when they are in doubt.[376]

These few examples demonstrate issues of principle. Airline staff are required to act as unofficial immigration officers, for which they have neither the authority nor the qualifications. This was an objection put forward by French representatives while discussing the Schengen Agreement.[377] It is rendered all the more paradoxical as most airline staff in the country of departure are nationals of that country and not of the country of arrival.

In effect, the fate of asylum-seekers is thus often being decided outside any formal and fair procedure. Moreover, the Chicago Convention on international transportation (7 December 1944, Trb 1973, 109) stipulates that the states which signed it: 'shall not fine operators in the event that passengers are found inadmissible, unless there is evidence to suggest that the carrier was negligent in taking precautions to the end that the passenger complied with the documentary requirements for entry into the receiving state'.[378] However, carriers' sanctions will probably remain.

UNHCR has made it clear that visas and airlines' sanctions imposed to stop asylum-seekers from leaving their own country or their country of first arrival contravene international legal principles. ECRE warns that 'it is contrary to international legal principles to impose entry visa requirements exclusively in order to prevent people from leaving their own country or country of first arrival in order to seek asylum'.[379] UNHCR, NGOs and other associations are trying to propose safeguards for asylum-seekers. In France a bill on sanctions against carriers mentions three cases in which a carrier would not be fined: if the company acted in good faith; if the passenger without valid entry documents is allowed entry to apply for asylum; and if the asylum request, although finally rejected, is considered by the authorities to be 'not manifestly unfounded'.[380] This seems to take some of UNHCR's recommendations into account.[381]

However, Amnesty International points out that airline staff are not equipped to determine whether the asylum claim will be deemed not manifestly unfounded. In effect safeguards turn airline staff into judges of asylum. And the question is then asked whether they are bound to observe Articles 31, 32 and 33 of the Geneva Convention should an asylum-seeker declare his intentions to them.[382]

Undocumented asylum-seekers

Asylum-seekers are frequently penalized for failing to be in possession of the required documents or visas. UNHCR produced a special report on this question for the Intergovernmental Consultations[383] (see Chapter 17 for further information on this body). In some countries asylum-seekers may be denied entry, kept in detention or their claim to asylum may be prejudiced by this factor.

In the UK it means that they are not allowed to stay during the appeal procedure and may be refused status under the new draft immigration rules appended to the Immigration Act.[384] In Denmark they can be returned at the border if they fail to produce proper documents (Procedures introduced by amendment in October 1986).[385]

This appears to be an infringement of the Geneva Convention (Art. 31) which stipulates that an asylum-seeker should not be penalized as long as he or she declares and regularizes his or her situation without delay.[386] It can be argued that such discrimination against one category of asylum-seekers contravenes the Geneva Convention.

This question deserves attention as the number of undocumented asylum-seekers is increasing for a variety of reasons. This is partly related to the measures taken by states: they find it difficult to obtain the documents in question and travel on false ones as it may be the only opportunity they have to flee from persecution; they destroy their papers before arrival; they try to conceal their route so that a country of 'first asylum' cannot be identified.[387]

International zones

A controversial concept is arising with regards to airport transit lounges. In many instances, portions of the airport are called 'international zones' and are deemed by states to be outside their sovereign territory. These states also consider that the 1951 Geneva Convention and other human rights conventions are not binding in these areas. Asylum-seekers are sometimes purposely confined to these zones so that they cannot apply for asylum. This may result in their being refouled to their country of origin where they fear persecution or to a third country which may not accept them.

Despite numerous cases won by complainants in the courts which reject the theory and practice of 'international zones', European countries continue to apply this concept to preclude asylum-seekers from having access to the appropriate authority to hand in their applications.[388] A growing object of concern to NGOs has been the detention of asylum-seekers in deplorable conditions, subject to summary procedures in airports, without access to legal advice or help from relevant NGOs.[389]

A colloquy on 'Human Rights without Frontiers' organized by the Council of Europe in Strasbourg in late 1989 considered a recommendation in favour of the presence of humanitarian organizations in the international zones of airports to render assistance to asylum-seekers in difficulty. NGOs have started to monitor the situation in airports and are trying to negotiate access to international zones.[390]

The Council of Europe's Parliamentary Assembly, after considering a report by investigators on visits to six airports (Roissy, Paris; Arlanda, Stockholm; Heathrow, London; Baraja, Madrid; Leonardo da Vinci, Rome; and Frankfurt, Germany), recommended that the European Convention on Human Rights and other international instruments be respected in reception centres and transit areas of airports and that UNHCR and NGOs be involved in the implementation of their provisions.[391] The French organization ANAFE (*Association Nationale d'Assistance aux Frontières pour les Etrangers*) held a conference sponsored by the Council of Europe on the status of frontier zones in the spring of 1992.

Safe countries of asylum
The notion of 'safe countries' was first developed in connection with so-called countries of first asylum. There is a variety of interpretations as to what constitutes a country of first asylum but also with regard to safe countries of first asylum. For most European countries it has meant any country which has signed the 1951 Convention, and the 1967 Protocol. However, some asylum-seekers have been sent back to a country which was not a signatory of these Conventions on the grounds that they had been given an undertaking that they would be respected.

NGOs and UNHCR have not rejected this concept, recognizing that it has some basis in the phraseology of the Convention which requires direct arrival from territories where life/freedom are threatened (Art. 31) but on only condition that a number of safeguards are implemented. The asylum-seeker should be able to enter and remain there, should be protected there against refoulement and treated in accordance with basic human standards, should not be subject to persecution or threats to safety and liberty and should have access to a durable solution.[392]

The latter prerequisite is the most difficult, as poor Third World countries might not be able to meet it. As a corollary to this trend, a number of bilateral or multiple agreements have been struck between countries for the readmission of aliens, such as the protocol between the Schengen states and Poland. Similar agreements between states are likely to increase in the future.[393]

Safe countries of origin
The concept of 'safe country of origin' has only recently been used as a legal device to prevent nationals of certain countries from obtaining asylum status or even from being admitted to an asylum procedure in receiving countries.[394] The Ad Hoc Immigration Group was reported by one source to be preparing a common list of 'safe' countries in a document for discussion by the European Council at Maastricht in December 1991.[395]

Several elements may motivate such a development. A list of safe countries can be used for alleviating the burden of procedural tasks, either leading to an automatic refusal of a number of asylum-seekers or sending them into an accelerated procedure track. It can constitute a clear signal discouraging nationals of certain countries from applying for asylum altogether. European states have also argued that it was meant to encourage democratization in the states of origin.

However, UNHCR has warned of the irregularities and risks involved in such a concept. It is inconsistent with several provisions of the 1951 Geneva Convention and 1967 Protocol: the individual character of refugee status and the subjective nature of fear of persecution; the geographical limitation thus de facto introduced; and the requirement not to discriminate according to the country of origin.[396] It would permit refoulement of certain nationals without exceptions. It would also infringe other human rights instruments, such as articles of the European Convention for the Protection of Human Rights, by excluding cases under which nationals of some countries classified as safe would still be in need of international protection.

Other, more fundamental, objections have been levelled at this concept. There is a risk of jeopardizing the human rights dimension of the issue through politicizing it; the decision to include a country in a safe list could be influenced by diplomatic relations between states, as excluding it might be deemed a condemnation of that state. Moreover, the volatile situation in some regions of the world might lead to massive blunders if a supposedly 'safe' country suffered a sudden setback.

Indeed, the definition of 'safe' is subject to controversy. For instance, the decision by Switzerland to deem Algeria and India 'safe' on the basis that they are 'democratic' countries or that there are internal flight alternatives available has been sharply criticized.[397] Finally, it is worth quoting UNHCR:

> *'It needs though to be reiterated that where it [the concept of safe country] serves to block any access to a status determination procedure, or where it results in serious inroads into procedural safeguards, it is to be strongly discouraged. In addition it must always to [sic] be recognised that decisions about safety are extremely difficult, given volatile human rights situations and the inherently biasing effect of political or foreign policy considerations.'*[398]

Accelerated procedure

The notion of an accelerated procedure has developed as a result of the considerable backlogs building up in the treatment of asylum applications. Several countries are already implementing such a procedure and it had been mentioned as a useful device in the European Commission White Paper on Asylum (*Avant-Projet de Directive*) dating back to 1988. The Intergovernmental Consultations are currently considering this issue. Accelerated procedures are intended to make it possible to reject non-refugees or those who do not need protection without delay and/or permit the speedy recognition of refugees and others requiring international protection. Accelerated procedure has been applied to three main categories:

1. 'Manifestly unfounded cases', however they may be defined. The accelerated procedure is most frequently used under this heading. It can take the shape of a pre-screening determining the admissibility of individual claims (Belgium);[399] it may lead to cases of *non-entrée en matière* as in Switzerland (Art. 16 Asylum Law) where decisions should be taken within six weeks for various reasons including the hiding of true identity, or being a national of a country declared by the Swiss government to be 'safe from persecution'; it can automatically channel a variety of categories of applicants such as those who obviously do not meet the Convention criteria, ie. putting forward economic reasons, having found protection in another state (not meeting Articles 1, 10, 15 of the Convention as in Portugal), avoiding a general state of emergency (Germany); in the UK it applies to those considered as undesirable for medical reasons, for committing an offence susceptible to extradition, because they are deemed to threaten public interest, etc.

Such a procedure may or may not offer an appeal mechanism and most frequently entails that the applicant does not have access to a full hearing.

2. 'Manifestly founded cases', as in Australia applying to torture and trauma victims and detention cases, or in France to those who 'manifestly fall within the status of refugees'.[400]

3. 'Special national groups', whether this be a positive or negative discrimination. In Canada it concerns the applications of Somalis, Iranians, Lebanese, Sri Lankans and Salvadoreans, the five predominant nationalities of asylum-seekers. In Italy it has taken place on an ad hoc basis as a 'special group determination' without personal hearing, adopted for Albanians in 1990 as *prima facie* refugees. In this context a list of safe countries can be instrumental in barring access to the procedure or sending nationals of those countries onto a fast track.

Refugee agencies and lawyers do not reject accelerated procedures. They clearly favour them where they are used positively. They warn of the inherent risks of error where they are used to exclude applicants from a full hearing, as 'few countries can be prescribed with confidence as non-refugee producing'.[401] Where negative presumptions bias the cases, good information and strong safeguards must guarantee that the merits of individual claims are examined.

The discussion over 'safe' countries and determination procedures raises again the question of individual versus group recognition. On the one hand, the granting of status based on national groups has displayed serious pitfalls which led to the adoption of a universal definition aimed at individuals in the 1951 Geneva Convention. On the other hand, individual fear of persecution thus defined presents other problems of principle or of a practical nature.

As long as asylum-seekers were relatively few and while the 1951 Convention was liberally applied, all refugees in need of protection were accommodated. But now that the numbers of asylum-seekers have increased, the established structures for processing applications do not seem able to cope with the demand; this results in enormous backlogs and long delays before a decision is made. Combined with tough immigration policies, it has led to very strict interpretations of the 1951 Convention, which in turn excludes refugees in need of protection for reasons which are not exactly those of individual fear of persecution as specified in the Convention.

Governments, UNHCR and NGOs are currently grappling with this problem. The 'safe' and, by corollary, 'unsafe' countries concept used within the framework of accelerated procedures can be understood in this context. It appears to provide a practical solution to the question of numbers but is questioned by UNHCR and NGOs, since such a group approach may jeopardize the awarding of protection to individuals.

UNHCR

Another area of concern for NGOs and organizations dealing with refugees has been UNHCR's proposals to restructure its European offices. One initiative would strengthen UNHCR representation in Central and Eastern Europe but this appears to be at the expense of UNHCR activities in Western Europe. In particular, the dismantling of UNHCR national representation is intended to be replaced by one or two strong regional offices in decision-making cities.

ECRE has pointed out that the urgent issues currently pertaining to refugees in Western Europe cannot be satisfactorily dealt with on a regional basis, as decisions affecting them (such as access to territory) are made by national governments.[402] NGOs also feel that such measures would send out the wrong message at a time when governments and public opinion are becoming increasingly unfavourable to refugees; UNHCR must be seen to maintain its interest in refugees in Western Europe and not give them a lower profile.[403]

17

CHALLENGING THE
POLITICAL BACKLASH

'...having thrown its doors wide open after the war to newcomers of a variety of ethnic origins who came here, individually or in groups, either to join the work of reconstruction and development or seeking in its lands refuge, freedom and justice, Europe today represents a much enriched ethnic and cultural picture... Like all great changes in history, this transformation is not without its problems and painful shocks. When the stresses of an economic and social crisis accompany the friction that inevitably results from the shaking down together of people differing in their ethnic origins, cultures and religious beliefs which may, indeed, by their content, tradition or particular political orientation be directly opposed, there is always a danger that a climate of intolerance or xenophobia may arise and occasionally prove alarming in its manifestations. Conscious of its responsibility, Europe must face this challenge frankly and clear-slightedly, with the kind of political integrity and moral courage which have marked the best hours of its history...'

– European Parliament, Committee of Enquiry into the Rise of Fascism and Racism in Europe, Report on the Findings of the Enquiry, December 1985.

I n the 1990s, a number of campaigns and initiatives are endeavouring to defend the right of asylum and to protect refugees in Western Europe. The issue has gained greater prominence among NGOs, the Churches and the legal profession and, to a lesser extent, among trade unions.

The Churches have set up several groups to deal with asylum (Conference of European Churches, World Council of Churches) and well-known Church leaders have protested against the treatment given to refugees. In the UK the Anglican Archbishop of Canterbury and the Catholic Archbishop of Westminster, each the national head of their respective Churches, wrote a joint letter to *The Times* protesting against the new Asylum Bill, and a 16,000-strong petition against it was presented, among others, by Catholic and Protestant Church leaders.[404]

Some trade unions have also criticized policies on refugees. In France the *Confédération Française Démocratique du Travail* (CFDT) has opposed sanctions against carriers and the involvement of airline staff in monitoring passengers' documents.

'Our trade union considers that airline staff should not have to become police auxiliaries... Finally, control at the point of departure constitutes a serious restriction to the right of asylum and an infringement of human rights'.[405]

NGOs and lawyers are repeatedly bringing test cases to national courts, the International Court at The Hague and the European Court of Human Rights, challenging national government decisions. Where refugees and asylum-seekers have been attacked, groups and vigils have been set up to protect them. The interests of rejected asylum-seekers also need to be protected, as many of them remain in European countries eking out a living in semi-clandestinity after waiting for years before a decision is taken on their status. A campaign on this issue was launched in 1991 in France by the *Réseau d'information et de solidarité pour les déboutés* (Information and solidarity network for rejected asylum-seekers).

A number of actions have also been taken on the margin of the law in order to challenge it. In the UK, a Manchester church harboured a Sri Lankan asylum-seeker, Viraj Mendes, for several months, only to be eventually stormed by the police. In Denmark, 120 Palestinians took sanctuary for two months in a church.[406] In Germany a group of supporters rescued some 70 asylum-seekers, victims of assaults in their hostel in Greifswald and moved them to Norderstedt in Schleswig-Holstein; they may have to face charges for doing so.[407]

The Swiss refugee support group (AAA), run by Dr Peter Zuber and his wife, was set up in 1984 to fight the country's rigid immigration laws; it finds temporary homes for refugees whose applications have been rejected. It is a powerful organization with 6000 members, offering refuge in some 200 homes; in case of prosecution those providing shelter risk prison and fines.

These initiatives have not reached the extent of the sanctuary movement in the USA but they may increase if the new policies being developed in Europe are judged to be too restrictive and unfair.

New initiatives

Refugee and immigration policy

Several countries are entirely reformulating their laws and policies on asylum. Although the general tendency is one of pure and simple restrictionism, as illustrated by the UK Asylum Bill, some countries are taking a more complex view of the issue.

New initiatives are always worth considering carefully as they may serve as models for other countries. For instance, both Sweden and Switzerland have produced a comprehensive document on refugees and immigration, and it appears that the Swiss paper was used as a basis for the Swedish one. 'Strategy for a Refugee and Asylum Policy for the Nineties' (Switzerland)[408] develops, over a hundred pages, a global approach to the question of refugees which takes on board developmental and ecological issues in the Third World. It considers the root causes of forced migration and proposes to intervene to defend human rights and reduce the sales of arms to state violators. It promotes aid to countries of first asylum and examines the relationship between asylum and immigration policies.

'A Comprehensive Refugee and Immigration Policy: Directives for a Government Committee' (Sweden)[409] is a preliminary paper setting out the premises for a more elaborate document yet to come. It considers the causes of migration and flight worldwide and points to a prospective increase in forced and voluntary migration as well as a supposed change in the character of refugee movements, now mostly attributed to generalized violence. This paper promotes a comprehensive and internationally coordinated approach and establishes the relationship between development assistance in poor countries and countries of first asylum, the defence of human rights worldwide, and a good reception and integration policy for refugees and migrants.

In both the Swiss and Swedish cases this new approach is justified by the claim that a new and comprehensive view is needed for refugee and asylum issues. In a lesser manner, a harbinger to this global and comprehensive approach could also be found in a document from the Federal Ministry of the Interior in Germany, 'Report by the Inter-Ministerial Working Group on a "Refugee Concept".'[410] It remains to be seen if these views will become more prevalent in Europe.

Both the EC and the Council of Europe appear to promote similar approaches. The EC has presented proposals at the UN General Assembly to introduce a permanent mechanism dealing with emergency assistance and to link such interventions to long-term development and human rights issues, thus focusing attention on the causes of flight.[411] The Committee of Ministers of the Council of Europe supported this proposal and at its meeting in September 1991 resolved to reinforce cooperation on all aspects of migration policy with the aim of 'improving respect for human rights and contributing to the economic, social and political development of the countries of origin'.[412]

NGOs have expressed mixed feelings about these initiatives. On the one hand, their global concern is seen as a positive departure from the narrow view expressed through the Schengen agreement and Dublin and Rome Conventions. For this reason, UNHCR has welcomed and encouraged such moves.[413] However, NGOs are worried by the way in which refugee and immigrant issues are, by implication, amalgamated, and the possibility of a relationship being established between the acceptance of some refugees and the situation in the labour market.[414]

Another dimension to these reconsidered policies is the inclusion of non-Convention refugees. The Swedish governmental committee recommended in 1991 that the new policy should give an unconditional right to stay not only to Convention refugees but also include, among others:

> 3. *Persons who cannot be rejected because it would violate Article 3 of the European Convention of Human Rights (protection against torture or inhuman or degrading treatment or punishment);*
> 4. *Persons who risk persecution... Article 14 of the Universal Declaration of Human Rights;*
> 5. *Persons who cannot be rejected because it would be in obvious contradiction to demands of humanity.*[415]

However, this proposal remains more restrictive than previous provisions, since others, such as persons with political and/or humanitarian reasons, including conscientious objectors, would only be accepted under a quota system.

In Switzerland the revised law has given the competence to the Federal Council to grant provisional admission collectively to refugees from violence, although it has not happened as yet.[416] The German document mentioned earlier defines as 'refugees for reasons of violence', distinct from 'Convention refugees' and 'economic refugees'

> *'persons who have left their country of origin due to justified fears of violence as a result of war, civil war or a similar situation in which there is frequent use of force. They do not enjoy the right of asylum... but they are, as a rule, not deported to their countries of origin for humanitarian reasons.'*[417]

In the Netherlands a new status is to be introduced with the Aliens Act currently being debated by Parliament in which a conditional permit to stay will be granted to persons who cannot be returned 'for reasons of government policy' (refugees from situation of turmoil).[418] The status of 'tolerated alien' (a temporary status) has been provisionally implemented from 1 January 1992.

However, only Convention refugees are ever mentioned in the harmonization initiatives, which leads to the question of whether provisions for other categories of refugee will simply be relegated to national government decisions. Moreover, the reception conditions attached to these alternative statuses tend, on the whole, to be less favourable than for Convention refugees.

Other international initiatives are perceived as contributing to a more concerted and positive treatment of refugee issues and an increasing number of European and international fora are including them in their considerations.

Intergovernmental Consultations
The Intergovernmental Consultations between UNHCR and governments were launched in the 1980s. In 1985 a meeting of 20 European states, convened to discuss the arrival of asylum-seekers in Europe, led to the setting up of the Intergovernmental Consultations on the Arrival of Asylum-seekers in Europe, comprising seven governments. The group now includes 14 governments (not all of them in Europe): Australia, Austria, Belgium, Canada, Denmark, Finland, France, Germany, Netherlands, Norway, Sweden, Switzerland, the UK and the USA. In June 1991 they set up an independent secretariat having diplomatic status with the UN and the technical back-up of UNHCR. Although government representatives at present come mostly from immigration departments, UNHCR is hoping that experts from other departments and from NGOs will be included.[419]

In their Strategy Platform they define as their main policy objectives:

> *'the facilitation of free movement whenever that is possible, the mitigation of causes which create forced movements, and the eventual harmonization of policy and action among states in regulating the movements of persons.'*[420]

While stressing that immigration and asylum policy pertain to national sovereignty and recognizing that states have responsibilities towards their own citizens, they reiterate the need to help refugees through international burden-sharing and adherence to the 1951 Geneva Convention and 1967 Protocol.

They identify two policy areas in which to implement their objectives. Through foreign and development policies they intend, among other aspects, to promote such cooperation with relevant countries as will strengthen their economies, further employment, improve standards of living and reinforce human rights, both promoting economic and social development and averting environmental degradation. They also pledge support for UNHCR.

In the area of asylum and migration policies they propose to exchange information on national asylum and aliens legislation and its implementation, the situation in relevant countries of origin and data on individual applicants, and on visa and transit visa policies. They present the 1990 Dublin Convention as the blueprint to be followed in identifying the responsibilities of states in handling requests for asylum, complete with the readmission principle. Among issues to be explored further they include the harmonization of asylum legislation, criteria and procedures in participating states and the establishment of safe areas in countries of origin.

European Community (EC)
Within the Community a discussion of EC competence on questions of asylum and the social rights of refugees has been brought to the fore and the European Commission has issued a Communication on Asylum (including a recommendation to harmonize conditions of reception). In June 1991 the European Council (EC Council of Ministers) approved German Chancellor Helmut Kohl's proposal that the Intergovernmental Conference on Political Union should consider the inclusion in the treaty of provisions to harmonize policy on asylum and also on immigration. A report was presented at Maastricht in December 1991.

The Conference on Security and Cooperation in Europe (CSCE).
This body brings together 52 (previously 35, 34 and 38) governments in Europe and North America to examine security and cooperation questions. It has not so far dealt with refugee issues but its Paris Charter (1990) lays down an important set of human rights objectives.[421] Its Copenhagen document (1990) states that the participating states will consult and cooperate in dealing with problems that might emerge as a result of the increased movement of persons, but it does not mention refugees as such.[422] NGOs are hoping that asylum-seekers and refugees will be considered positively in future.

Conference of Ministers

Finally, the Conference of Ministers on the Movement of Persons from Central and Eastern European Countries, consisting of European and non-European states, took place in Vienna on 24-5 January 1991 with the participation of the European Commission and UNHCR. It plans to promote permanent cooperation to settle questions of immigration and refugees in Europe, and stated its commitment to the main relevant international instruments (including the 1951 Convention, the 1967 Protocol and the European Convention on Human Rights, among others).[423]

The discussion is not closed; policies are still in the making and the outcome is not clear. However, it is certain that asylum-seekers and refugees will remain a major item on the European and international agenda for a considerable time. In the long run, it is only when positive efforts are made to deal with the root causes of refugee exodus that real progress can be made.

CONCLUSIONS

THE FUTURE FOR REFUGEES
IN EUROPE

This book has highlighted some of the many issues surrounding the current situation faced by refugees in Europe – the reasons for their existence, the international legal conventions which determines their status, the national laws and institutions which govern their daily lives and their prospects for the future.

What the book cannot do, by its very nature, is tell all the unique stories of the individual refugees – the tales of torture and persecution, the long wait for asylum and acceptance, the loneliness of exile, and, in a few cases, the triumph over adversity and the return to a liberated land. Yet it is their collective voices which provides the most eloquent advocacy for a generous response by European states to their asylum claims. But is Europe ready to listen to them calmly and open-mindedly?

It is in the nature of refugee movements for numbers to rise and fall. The numbers of refugees grew throughout the 1980s and will probably continue to grow in the 1990s. Today there are over half a million asylum-seekers in Western Europe. In addition for the first time in half a century Europe is generating substantial numbers of its own refugees and potential refugees as a result of civil wars, the dissolution of states, ethnic or religious tension exacerbated by economic distress and abuse of human rights.

Over the last decade the restrictions and barriers to the entry of asylum-seekers have tightened in all Western European states. In the immediate aftermath of the collapse of Communist regimes in Eastern Europe, there was some loosening of restrictions. But today these states, some of whom are also the creators of asylum-seekers, are also resorting to restrictive practices, frequently under the influence of Western European governments.

Furthermore in almost every European country there has been consistent attempts to discredit and deprive refugees of their dignity in the eyes of the majority population. Sometimes extreme political parties lead the call to limit, to refuse or to deport asylum-seekers, attempting to whip up a hysterical outcry against an easy political target, sometimes governments themselves take the lead, frequently for cynical political gain, a call echoed and amplified by sections of the media.

Yet there is every indication that unless European governments take urgent and coordinated action to defend the human rights of asylum-seekers, refugees and displaced persons, the situation can only worsen. The specific reasons for refugee flight and the processes which governs their recognition are frequently complex but the root causes are often devastatingly simple.

Tackling root causes of refugees

Refugees are created by many factors but, above all, by serious and gross violations of civil, political, economic, social and cultural rights. Lasting solutions can only be found by tackling the root causes of these problems. It is essential to work for ecologically and economically sustainable development, allied to civil and political rights, and to achieve economic, social and cultural rights, particularly minority rights.

The EC and other European bodies should individually and jointly make a substantial contribution to appropriate development programmes in the countries of the South and in the newly emerging democracies of Eastern Europe. Development assistance and trade should be clearly linked to the active promotion and observance of human rights, including the respect of minority rights, and the diffusion of tensions leading to conflicts. These measures need to be implemented now, for experience shows that once conflicts become violent, it is almost always too late for mediation to be effective.

There should be increased financial support by European governments for refugee programmes outside Europe. Support should be provided to UNHCR to provide basic needs (food, safe water supplies, housing) while aid should be given to host states and refugee organizations to provide both short-term welfare assistance and long-term development support. Regional solutions should be sought, where possible involving local communities.

Nevertheless, there needs to be recognition that there are some situations so extreme, where abuse is frequent and daily life so violent, that, at least in the short-term, outside pressure can provide no amelioration. Under these circumstances, refugees will be inevitable. European governments must act with all urgency to protect refugees, whether in Europe or elsewhere.

Strengthening international standards

There is an absolute need for all European states to ratify international legal standards concerning refugees. Over the past few years more states, especially from Eastern Europe, have signed the 1951 Geneva Convention and the 1967 Protocol. All those remaining states who have not signed should be encouraged to do so. Even more important however is an adherence to the principles of the conventions and a willingness for governments to act in the spirit of humanity.

European regional bodies with human rights responsibilities should give higher priority to refugee issues. Such bodies include the Conference on Security and Cooperation in Europe (CSCE), the Council of Europe, the European Parliament, the European Court of Human Rights and sub-regional groups such as the Nordic Council.

As a matter of urgency there should be public discussions and reviews on the situation of refugees, displaced persons and potential refugees in and from Central and Eastern Europe and the ex-USSR. These should be designed to support efforts to mediate where tensions exist, to promote human and minority rights and to provide support for refugees and internally displaced peoples. That these mechanisms need to take effect earlier and to be strengthened can be seen from the tragic situation in the former Yugoslavia.

Governments, inter-governmental organizations, EC institutions as well as NGOs should ensure that issues relating to refugees are raised regularly in UN human rights bodies and that issues are considered in country and thematic reports. It is important not to forget concerns about asylum-seekers in democratic European states and if these states act in unprincipled and inhumane ways then other governments and NGOs should not hesitate to criticize them in the international arena for failing to honour their international agreements.

European practices on refugees

The 1951 Convention and 1967 Protocol, together with all other international human rights instruments to which European states are signatories, were created by governments and set fundamental human rights standards which European governments should observe in their practices and treatment of refugees and asylum-seekers. These standards should be interpreted in a coherent, consistent and open manner, following the principles of justice, good government and fair administration.

European harmonization should not be used as a reason for further restrictions on refugees or asylum-seekers. There should be an active search for a coherent European system, which is just, equitable and consistent with international legal standards. All European states should aim to implement the most generous standards, rather than the most restrictive ones.

Unfortunately many of the details of the harmonization process have been carried out in secrecy and are implemented in an underhand manner. Because so much of the new legislation is technically complex, it is difficult to assess the full impact it will have on asylum-seekers. It is essential that parliamentarians, lawyers and NGOs should be invited to contribute to the harmonization process and that all deliberations and decisions are published and are freely available.

In the 1980s many European states have placed airline carriers in the forefront of attempts to control refugee flows. Not only is this wrong in principle, but it has lead to considerable injustice, sometimes even ill-treatment and torture, for individual asylum-seekers who have been denied entry to a European state or summarily deported to their home country or to a third country. Visa restrictions on some countries and the creation of 'international zones' at airports have a similar effect.

Treatment meted out to individual asylum-seekers at times can be confusing and inconsistent, and, at worst, can be inhumane and degrading. Governments should ensure that from the first contact individual asylum-seekers should be treated equitably, courteously and within the framework of specially established procedures by qualified and impartial personnel. Under no circumstances should asylum-seekers be routinely treated as 'immigrants in disguise'. Immigration control policies must never deny the right of an asylum-seeker to seek asylum from persecution.

All those claiming asylum should have their individual cases examined fairly, independently and in a way consistent with due process of law. Where necessary, a competent and impartial interpreter should be made available. Nor should the asylum-seeker be isolated from family and friends, legal advice or community support. Vulnerable groups, such as women, children, the elderly and the disabled need special consideration. Asylum-seekers from all states should be given equal treatment and groups should not be automatically favoured or discriminated against because of their nationality.

Asylum-seekers should not be treated as virtual criminals and should not be detained or subject to unreasonable restrictions in their movements. The entire procedure from arrival of asylum-seekers to the final decision on their status should be as short as is consistent with following a full and fair process of law.

Not all asylum-seekers will be formally recognized as refugees under the Geneva Convention. However, legal protection should be granted generously by European states to persons who, although they may not meet the criteria of the 1951 Convention and the 1967 Protocol, cannot safely return to their country of nationality. There should also be a coherent European policy on rejected asylum-seekers, to prevent placing individuals at risk and to respect their dignity as individual human beings. All rejected asylum-seekers have a right to a detailed account of the criteria and reasons for the decision, and a right of appeal against the decision, consistent with normal legal norms, must be available.

Eastern Europe

Faced with the sudden upsurge in asylum-seekers from Eastern Europe, the West is in danger of creating a 'fortress Europe' with the old Iron Curtain rebuilt by the West to keep out migrants. Eastern European countries, with their recent history of repression and their avowed aim of joining the West as quickly as possible, have been loath to close their own countries to the new phenomenon of transient migrants but they do not have the legislation and administration to cope with them satisfactorily.

In the short-term, efforts need to be made to inform Eastern Europeans as to the real situation in the West regarding current policies on labour migration. In so far as there may be movements of persons from Eastern Europe not based on refugee-related reasons, long-term aid is needed to improve the economic and political conditions in all countries so that the great majority of the population have a positive incentive to remain there.

There is possibly also a need to change traditional labour migration policies in Western Europe. One solution might be to establish labour migration on a short-term basis combined with vocational training so that returnees can help build their own societies. A German-Romanian project on these lines is intended to be extended to other Eastern European states, particularly Poland and Bulgaria, and possibly also the successor states to the USSR. There is potential for such measures in the increasing European cooperation on migration which includes the Eastern European states.

But, to date, political consensus has been sadly lacking in the fields of conflict prevention, resolution and mediation. The international community, especially the Western European states, must persist in the development of political mechanisms designed to defuse destructive conflicts, like the Yugoslav civil war, which cause large-scale forced migration. Such mechanisms are inevitably difficult to implement but without them the situation can only deteriorate further.

The refugee contribution

All too often refugees are portrayed as a burden on the host society, with nothing worthwhile to contribute. Yet an objective analysis shows that refugees can and do make real and lasting economic and cultural contributions in their new countries. However rather than receiving support and encouragement, refugees frequently face enormous obstacles.

Recognized refugees are entitled to the same economic, social and cultural rights as nationals, to subsistence, housing, education, training and employment, language and religious beliefs. They have special needs for their long-term development, including practical support in language training, education programmes and employment retraining and for social, medical and psychological programmes geared to their needs.

Refugees must be guaranteed civil and political rights to practise political activities, as long as these do not infringe the laws of their host country. Without these guaranteed rights, the refugee is prevented from living as a full member of their new society. Refugees are nearly always minorities in their host country and their rights as minorities must be respected through support for their own languages, culture and way of life.

The refugee contribution needs to be publicly acknowledged. Government bodies, politicians, public figures, NGOs and the media should work to spread accurate information on the reasons why refugees flee and the problems they face. Racist and xenophobic incitement to hatred against refugees, whether by the media or by members of the public, should be combated by legal mechanisms.

Finally refugees themselves should be assisted and encouraged to organize their own community associations and to speak on their own behalf. It is often a deeply painful process – to speak of torture and mistreatment, of the death of family and friends, of the loss of home and country. Yet by speaking out they can assist themselves to come to terms with the past and to reach beyond to the non-refugee population, to tell their stories and to add to the struggle for justice and human rights.

FOOTNOTES

Some abbreviations used in these references

ANAFE	Association Nationale d'Assistance aux Frontières pour les Etrangers.
ATA	Albanian Telegraph Association.
BRC	British Refugee Council.
BTA	Bulgarian Telegraph Association.
CDFT	Confédération Française Démocratique du Travail.
CDMG	Comité Européen sur les Migrations.
CEI	Centre for Employment Initiatives.
CIEMI	Centre d'Information et d'Etudes sur les Migrations Internationales.
CRER	Centre for Research in Ethnic Relations, Warwick University.
CSTK	Czechoslovak News Service.
DPA	Deutsche Press Agenz.
ECRE	European Consultation on Refugees and Exiles.
FTDA	France Terre d'Asile.
GDM	Groupement pour les Droits des Minorités.
JPRS	US State Department Press Review Service.
MNS	Migration News Sheet.
MTI	Hungarian Telegraph Association.
PAP	Polish Press Agency.
RFE	Radio Free Europe.
SCLRAE	Standing Conference of Local and Regional Authorities of Europe.
SSAE	Service Social d'Aide aux Emigrants.
SWB (BBC)	Summary of World Broadcasts of British Broadcasting Corporation.
UNHCR	United Nations High Commissioner for Refugees.
ZDWF	Zentrale Dokumentationstelle der Freien Wohlfahrtspflege für Flüchtlinge.

[1] Marrus M.R., *The Unwanted: European Refugees in the Twentieth Century*, OUP, New York, 1985.

[2] Hope Simpson, J., *The Refugee Problem: Report of a Survey*, OUP, London, 1939, p.230.

[3] *Ibid.*, pp.4-5.

[4] Coles, G.J.L., *Solutions to the problem of refugees and the protection of refugees: A background study prepared for the Round Table on Durable Solutions and the Protection of Refugees*, convened by the office of the UNHCR in conjunction with the International Institute of Humanitarian Law, Geneva, 1989.

[5] Gallagher, D., *The Era of Refugees: The Evolution of the International Refugee System*, Refugee Policy Group, Washington, 1989, p.4.

[6] Marrus, M.R., *op. cit.*, pp.40-50 and Hope Simpson, J., *op. cit.*, pp.29-61. For further information on specific groups also see MRG Reports, *The Armenians* and *Minorities in The Balkans* and Rapports du Groupement pour les Droits des Minorités (GDM), Yacoub, J., *Les Assyro Chaldéens: Un peuple oublié de l'histoire*, Paris, 1987.

[7] A wide variety of figures were cited and, as Hope Simpson, notes 'they were originally made at a time of obvious and ample room for error', *op. cit.*, p.80.

[8] Gallagher, D., *op. cit.*, p.6.

[9] Marrus, M.R., *op. cit.*, pp.86-87, Gallagher, D., op. cit., p.7.

[10] *Ibid.*, p.8.

[11] Costa-Lascoux, J., 'Réfugiés et demandeurs d'asile en Europe' in *Revue Européenne des Migrations Internationales*, Vol.3, No. 1 et 2, 3e trimestre 1987, pp.240-241.

[12] Gallagher, D., op. cit, p.13.

[13] Wasserstein, B., *Britain and the Jews of Europe*, OUP, Oxford, 1988, p.8; Coles, G.J.L., *op. cit.*, p.34.

[14] *Ibid.*, p.34.

[15] Gallagher, D., *op. cit.*, p.15; Marrus, M.R., *op. cit.*, pp. 170-172; Coles, G.J.L., *op. cit.*, pp.38-40.

[16] Marrus, M.R., *op. cit.*, p.178.

[17] Proudfoot, M.J., *European Refugees: 1939-52*, Faber and Faber, London, 1957, p.21.

[18] Marrus, M.R., *op. cit.*, p.330.

[19] Gallagher, D., *op. cit.*, p.24.

[20] For instance, *Le Monde*, 15/1/88, reports the burning of 138,000 copies of the January issue of *Refugees*, the UNHCR magazine, on the orders of Jean-Pierre Hocke, the then High Commissioner, and the protest that ensued. It was alleged that this decision was motivated by the desire not to offend the government of the Federal Republic of Germany whose policy on refugees was discussed in the issue. According to the *Guardian* (1/8/90), the US administration has warned the UNHCR that Washington might withdraw funds for certain refugee projects if UNHCR became involved with the British mandatory repatriation scheme of Vietnamese refugees, 'boat people', from Hong Kong.

[21] Melander, G., 'The two refugee definitions', Report No.4, Raoul Wallenberg Institute, Lund, 1987, pp.9-22.

[22] United Nations High Commission for Refugees (UNHCR), Geneva, 1979.

[23] Factors influencing the interpretation of the Convention will be examined later in this book.

24 Casella, A., 'Asylum-seekers in Europe: a humanitarian quandary', in *The World Today*, November 1988, pp.187-191.
25 Signatories to the Convention only: Madagascar, Monaco, Mozambique. Signatories to the Protocol only: Swaziland, USA, Venezuela.
26 Austria, Belgium, Bulgaria, Czechoslovakia, Cyprus, Denmark, Finland, France, Germany, Greece, Hungary, Iceland, Republic of Ireland, Italy, Liechtenstein, Luxembourg, Malta, Netherlands, Norway, Poland, Portugal, San Marino, Spain, Sweden, Switzerland, Turkey, UK.
27 Chemillier-Gendreau, M., 'Le concept de réfugié en droit international et ses limites', in *Actes*, No.40, *Droit d'asile et réfugiés*, pp.13-17.
28 Paludan, A., 'The new refugees in Europe', in *Summary of the Report on Problems of Refugees and Exiles in Europe*, Geneva, International University Exchange Fund on behalf of the Working Group on Refugees and Exiles in Europe, 1974, pp.3-47.
29 Zarjevski, M., *A Future Preserved: International Assistance to Refugees*, Pergamon Press/UNHCR, Oxford, 1988.
30 41 African states are signatory to the OAU Convention.
31 Ecumenical Consultation on Asylum and Protection, Mission Statement, Zurich, 27/4/86 to 2/5/86.
32 Cels, J., *A Liberal and Humane Policy for Refugees and Asylum-seekers: Still a Realistic Policy Option?*, OUP, December 1986, p.35.
33 Bettati, M., *L'asile politique en question*, Paris, PUF, 1985.
34 Soulier, G., 'Droit d'asile et souveraineté de l' Etat' in *Actes* No.40, *Droit d'asile et réfugiés*, pp.19-21, p.20.
35 Sweden, Denmark, the Netherlands (B status is no longer granted in the Netherlands), Belgium, Germany and Switzerland have or have had these categories.
36 Goodwin-Gill, G. S., *The Refugee in International Law*, Clarendon Press, Oxford, 1983.
37 Paludan, A., *op. cit.*, pp.3-47, p.7.
38 Council of Europe, Parliamentary Assembly, *Report on the situation of de facto refugees*, 5/8/75, Doc. 3642, p.11.
39 Hocke, J-P., 'Beyond humanitarianism: the need for political will to resolve today's refugee problem', Refugee Studies Programme, Joyce Pearce Memorial Lecture, Oxford University, 29/11/86.
40 Kunz, E.F., 'The refugees in flight: kinetic models and forms of displacement', *International Migration Review*, 1973, Vol.7, No.2, pp.125-146.
41 Zolberg, A., et al., *Escape from Violence; Conflict and the Refugee Crisis in the Developing World*, OUP, Oxford, 1989, p.68.
42 Hathaway, J.C., 'The evolution of refugee status in international law: 1920-1950', *International and Comparative Law Quarterly* (ICLQ 33), 1984.
43 *Ibid.*
44 Vetter, H.O., *Report on the Right of Asylum*, European Parliament, 23/2/87, p.9.
45 Rudge, P., 'Fortress Europe', in *World Refugee Survey 1986*, US Committee for Refugees, Washington, 1987.
46 The vast majority of refugees in Europe are in the northern parts of the continent. For convenience 'Europe' in this instance will be used to comprise the following countries except where otherwise indicated: Austria, Belgium, Denmark, France, Germany, the Netherlands, Norway, Sweden, Switzerland, and the United Kingdom (UK).

[47] Casella, A., *op. cit.*

[48] Widgren, J., *Data on asylum-seekers in Europe in the context of intercontinental migration*, UNHCR, Memorandum, 24/3/88.

[49] Widgren, J., 'Asylum until the year 2000', Refugee Conference in Malmö, Sweden, 5/12/88, p.10.

[50] *Ibid.*

[51] *Le Monde*, 28/6/88.

[52] ECRE, *Report of Bi-annual General Meeting*, Budapest, 7-9/3/91.

[53] Table 3, Asylum applications in Europe (except southern Europe) and Canada by countries of origin of applicants in 1988. Tables from J. Widgren.

[54] *Documentation-Réfugiés*, No.50, 17-26/9/88, Annexe, pp.9-10.

[55] Countries included are: Austria, France, West Germany, Netherlands, Norway, Switzerland and UK. Source: UNHCR documents and ECRE.

[56] Widgren, J., Data on asylum-seekers, op. cit., p.3.

[57] Vetter, H.O., *op. cit.*, p.22.

[58] ECRE, *Report of Bi-annual General Meeting*, Budapest, 7-9/3/91.

[59] ECRE, Participants' meeting, October 1988.

[60] Von Arnim, R., *Présentation, UNHCR délégué régional auprès des pays du Benelux, et des institutions européennes, lors de la réunion du groupe central des négociations de Schengen le*, 25/10/91.

[61] ECRE, *Towards Harmonisation of Refugee Policies in Europe? A Contribution to the Discussion*, ECRE, London, October 1988, p.5.

[62] Quoted in Rudge, P., 'The spirit: historical and social perspectives. The failure of the spirit', *The Refugee Crisis, British and Canadian Responses*, International Symposium, 4-7/1/89, London, p.4.

[63] Soulier, G., 'Le respect du droit d'asile, preuve et garant du droit démocratique', France Terre d'Asile, *La Lettre d'Information*, No.65, June 1987, pp.8-18.

[64] ECRE, Participants' meeting, October 1988.

[65] ECRE, Participants' meeting, March 1988.

[66] ECRE, Participants' meeting, April 1989.

[67] *Ibid.*

[68] ECRE, Participants' meeting, October 1986.

[69] ECRE, Participants' meeting, April 1989.

[70] ECRE, Participants' meeting, October 1988.

[71] ECRE, Participants' meeting, April 1989.

[72] *Ibid.*

[73] Vetter, H.O., *op. cit.*, p.12.

[74] *Ibid.*

[75] Danish Refugee Council, *The Role of Airline Companies in the Asylum Procedure*, Copenhagen, 1988.

[76] *The Independent*, 25/8/89.

[77] ECRE, Participants' meeting, October 1988.

[78] 'Refugees – Britain's shame', *Searchlight*, July 1989, No.169, p.17.

[79] ECRE, Participants' meeting, October 1988.

[80] Morgado, C., 'The role of Members of Parliament in Immigration cases', Policy Papers in *Ethnic Relations* No.14, CRER, University of Warwick, UK, 1989.

[81] Rudge, P. (Secretary-General of ECRE), Interview, August 1989.

[82] France Terre d'Asile, 'Expulsions du 7 Decembre 1987 (Iraniens, Turcs et Kurdes de Turquie)', *La Lettre d'Information*, Numéro spécial, March 1988.

[83] Amnesty International, *Amnesty International's Concerns in Western Europe*, October 1986 to March 1987, SF 87 10 110, EUR 03/01/87, April 1987.

[84] ECRE, Participants' meeting, October 1988, p.9.

[85] ZDWF – *Schriftenreihe* Nr. 20 Elena/ZDWF: European Lawyers Workshop on detention, choice of residence and freedom of movement of asylum-seekers and refugees, May 1987.

[86] ECRE, Participants' meeting, April 1989.

[87] Cohen, R., 'The detention of asylum-seekers in the UK' in Joly, D., and Cohen, R., (Eds), *Reluctant Hosts: Europe and its Refugees*, Gower, Aldershot, 1989, pp.145- 162, p.148.

[88] ECRE, Participants' meeting, October 1988, p.11.

[89] ECRE, *Report of Bi-annual General Meeting*, October 1991.

[90] *Ibid.*

[91] ZDWF, *op. cit.*

[92] Vetter, H.O., *op. cit.*, p.12.

[93] *Ibid.*

[94] ECRE, Participants' meeting, October 1988, p.21.

[95] ECRE, European Lawyers Workshop on the implementation of article 1a of the Geneva Convention, Paris, 4-5/5/85.

[96] *Le Monde*, quoting Tiberghien, 19/4/88.

[97] Cohen, R., *op. cit.*, p.148.

[98] Vetter, H.O., *op. cit.*, p.24.

[99] Rudge, P., Interview, August 1989.

[100] Vetter, *op. cit.*, p.16.

[101] *Ibid.*, p.18. More recent figures show some changes.

[102] ECRE, Participants' meeting, October 1988.

[103] *Ibid.*

[104] ECRE, Participants' meeting, April 1989.

[105] Cels, J., *op. cit.*, p.139.

[106] ECRE, Participants' meeting, April 1989.

[107] Rapport UNHCR/FTDA, September 1987.

[108] Soulier, G., *op. cit.*, pp.19-21, p.20.

[109] Collection of International Instruments concerning Refugees,Geneva, UNHCR, 1979, p.102.

[110] Council of Europe, Parliamentary Assembly, *Report on living and working conditions of refugees and asylum-seekers*, Rapporteur Mr Böhm, 26/3/85.

[111] Joly, D., 'Britain and its Refugees: The Case of the Chileans', in *Migration*, 1987, Vol.1, pp.91-108, p.97.

[112] Phillips, A., 'Employment as a key to settlement' in Joly and Cohen, *op. cit.*, pp.133-145, p.136.

[113] Jones, P., *Vietnamese refugees, a study of their reception and resettlement in the United Kingdom*, Research and Planning Unit Paper 13, Home Office, London, 1982, p.49.

[114] Jaeger, G., 'The Integration of Refugees in Europe', UNHCR, 1983 *Seminar on the Integration of Refugees in Europe*, Geneva, 12-15/9/83, p.15.

[115] Joly and Cohen, *op. cit.*

[116] Castro, N., 'Elderly Refugees and their problems', unpublished, London, BRC, March 1989.

[117] Vasquez, A., et Araujo, A.M., *Exils Latino-Américains: La Malédiction d'Ulysse*, CIEMI L'Harmattan, Paris, 1988.

[118] ADRI, *Le devenir des réfugiés et demandeurs d'asile ayant séjourné dans les centres provisoires d'hébergement*, Note de synthèse, Paris, ADRI, n.d. p.6.

[119] Reid, J., and Strong, T., *Torture and Trauma*, Cumberland College of Health Sciences, Sydney, 1987.

[120] Vasquez and Araujo, *op. cit.*, and Vasquez, A., 'The Process of Transculturation: Exiles in France', in Joly and Cohen, *op. cit.*, pp.125-133.

[121] Khamsay Soukhavong, P., 'Réflexions sur les problèmes rencontrés en France par les réfugiés du Sud-Est asiatique,' *Migrants Formation*, La Formation des Réfugiés, No Spécial, No. 41-42, October 1980, pp.26-29.

[122] Lexa, F., 'Les réfugiés aujourd'hui' in *Vie Sociale*, No.1, January 1985, pp.3-9, p.8.

[123] Paludan, A., *op. cit.*, p.27.

[124] Joly, D., *Refugees from Vietnam in Birmingham: Community, Voluntary Agency and the Role of Local Authority*, Research Paper No.9, CRER, University of Warwick, 1988.

[125] Field, S., *Resettling Refugees: the Lessons of Research*, A Home Office Research and Planning Unit Report, HMSO, London, 1987.

[126] Council of Europe, CDMG, *Echanges de vues concernant la condition sociale des réfugiés*, Strasbourg, 17/3/88.

[127] Council of Europe, SCLRAE, 19th Session (Strasbourg 16-18/10/84), Opinion No.25 (1984) (1) on reception of refugees and asylum seekers by local authorities.

[128] UNHCR, Report of Social Services Workshop, Europe, Geneva, 18-21/6/84, p.4.

[129] Council of Europe, CDMG, *op. cit.*

[130] Jaeger, G., *op. cit.*, pp.14-18; Council of Europe, Parliamentary Assembly, *Report on living and working conditions*, op. cit., p.6.

[131] Centre for Employment Initiatives, *A Report on the Employment Situation of Refugees*, prepared for the UNHCR, CEI, London, 1984, p.3.

[132] UNHCR, *Follow-up to the 1983 Seminar on the Integration of Refugees in Europe, Report on the Second Meeting of the Contact Group* (Geneva 6/11/84), 21/1/85, p.4.

[133] Jones, P., *op. cit.*, p.16.

[134] Santa Cruz, M.J., 'Refugees from South East Asia in Spain: the Challenge of Hope' in Joly and Cohen, op. cit., pp.54-66.

[135] Sayers, R., 'Resettling Refugees: the Dutch Model' in Joly and Cohen, *op. cit.*, pp.19-39.

[136] Council of Europe, CDMG, *op. cit.*

[137] Joly, D., *op. cit.*

[138] Field, S., *op. cit.*, p.39.

[139] Lohrmann, R., 'Un rapport du Conseil de l'Europe sur les mesures sociales prises par les pays membres en faveur des réfugiés politiques', *Hommes et Migrations*, Vol.32, No.1010, 15/4/81, année, pp.3-38.

[140] Phillips, A., 'Conclusions', *Training and Employment Provisions for Refugees in Europe, Report of the Surrey Conference*, London, BRC-ECRE, March 1988, pp.13-17, p.15.

[141] 'Une formation d'adaptation pour des assistants sociaux latino-américains' *Migrants-Formation*, No.41-42, October 1980, pp.77-78.

[142] Phillips A., in Joly and Cohen, *op. cit.*, p.136.

[143] 'Pour l'insertion des réfugiés: création d'une entreprise Troyes', France Terre d'Asile, *La Lettre d'Information*, No.64, March 1987, pp.19-25.

[144] Centre for Employment Initiatives, *op. cit.*, p.43.

[145] Jordana, M.C., and Sanchez Pardo, L., 'Spanish Resettlement Programmes' in Cohen and Joly, *op. cit.*, pp.176-183.

[146] Centre for Employment Initiatives, *op. cit.*

[147] Vasquez, A., 'La scolarisation des adolescents latino-américains éxilés' *Migrants-Formation*, No.41-42, October 1980, pp.104-107.

[148] Lohrmann, R., *op. cit.*

[149] Cimade-Information No.11-12, 11/12/83.

[150] SSAE, La Formation des Réfugiés, Paris, December 1986.

[151] Lohrmann, R., *op. cit.*

[152] Council of Europe, SCLRAE, 19th Session, *op. cit*, p.2; *Migrants-Formation*, No.41-42, October 1980, pp.104-107.

[153] Field, S., *op. cit.*

[154] *Ibid.*, p.48-49.

[155] UNHCR, *op. cit.*, p.4.

[156] Council of Europe, *op. cit.*, p.3, 131.

[157] UNHCR, *op. cit.*

[158] Joint Working Group for Refugees from Chile in Britain, *Refugees from Chile: an Interim Report*, JWGR, London, 1975.

[159] UNHCR, *op. cit.*, p.16.

[160] *The Times*, 13/2/87.

[161] *The Times*, 7/3/87.

[162] *The Guardian*, 17/3/87.

[163] ECRE, October 1988, *op. cit.*

[164] International Social Services, Unaccompanied Minor Refugees in European Resettlement Countries, Seminar held by ISS, German Branch and ECRE, 13-16/3/84, Frankfurt am Main.

[165] Figures from *The Times Atlas of World History*, ed Barraclough, G., Times Books, 1978, p274.

[166] Moussalli, M., Director of International Protection of UNHCR, at the 8th Seminar on Contempoarary International Humanitarian Law and Current Human Rights Issues in Europe, Bucharest, 27-30/6/91.

[167] Tanjug, 15/12/91, SWB EE/1258 C1/6, 18/12/91.

[168] Poulton, H., *The Balkans: Minorities and States in Conflict*, Minority Rights Publications, June 1991.

[169] *Ibid.*

[170] Schopflin, G., and Poulton, H., *Romania's Ethnic Hungarians*, MRG Report, 1990.

[171] *The Times*

[172] Poulton, *op. cit.*

[173] Jenny, R., Director of Operations for the International Office for Migration, at Bucharest seminar, as of note 166.

[174] Moussalli, M. as of note 166.

[175] Sztuchlik, R., President and Secretary General of the Hungarian Red Cross, at Bucharest seminar as of note 166.

[176] *Ibid.*

[177] CTK, 25/1/91, SWB EE/0981 B/6, 28/1/91.

[178] CSTK 16/3/92, SWB EE/1332 B/10 18/3/92.

179 *Gazeta Wyborcza*, 19/12/90 in JPRS-EER-91-018, 11/2/91.
180 'Uncensored Poland', *Weekly Calendarium*, 23/5/91.
181 *The Economist*, London, March 1991.
182 Tanjug, 11/3/91 and 18/3/91, SWB EE/1021 B/4, 15/3/91, and EE/1025 A2/3, 20/3/91.
183 Tanjug, 20/1/92, SWB EE/1284 C1/4, 22/1/92.
184 Albanian Ministry of the Interior, ATA, 13/2/91, SWB EE/0997 B/3, 15/2/91.
185 BTA, 12/3/92 SWB EE/1330, A2/2, 15/3/92.
186 Ursu, D.V., Romanian Minister of the Interior, Bucharest Conference as of note 166.
187 Albanian Radio, Tirana, 12/1/92, SWB, EE/1277 B/1, 14/1/92.
188 BTA, 26/5/91, SWB, EE/1083 B/6, 28/5/91.
189 Perry, D.M., 'Minorities and Bulgarian Nationalism', RFE Vol.2, No.50, 13/12/91.
190 Poulton, *op. cit.*
191 BTA, 11/4/91, SWB EE/1048 B/5.
192 'Zabarnalite ot Turtsiya balgarski grazhdanishte badat obezeshtetni', *Demokratsiya*, Sofia, 2/8/91.
193 Poulton, *op. cit.*
194 Rompres, 4/1/92, SWB EE/0964 B/8, 8/1/91.
195 *Ibid.*
196 Rompres, 29/1/91, SWB EE/0985 B/8, 1/2/91.
197 Zurcher, G., Vice-Director of the Federal Office for Refugees in Switzerland, at Bucharest Conference as of note 166. Interestingly Zurcher stated that there were no Hungarian, Czechoslovak or Polish refugees in Switzerland, reflecting the more optimistic view of their own societies by young people in those countries as opposed to those in the Balkans.
198 Kokan, J., 'Poles Scramble for fake passports to the West', *Sunday Times*, London, 7/10/90.
199 *US State Department Report on Human Rights*, 1985, p.1079.
200 McQuaid, D., 'The Growing Assertiveness of Minorities', *RFE* Vol. 2, No. 50, 13/12/91.
201 *Ibid.*
202 Reuters 1991 (no date).
203 *Ibid.*
204 Prague Radio for Abroad, 22/3/90, SWB EE/0721 A3/1, 24/3/90.
205 CSTK, 18/12/91, SWB EE/1260 B/7, 20/12/91.
206 BTA, 19/6/91, SWB EE/1109 A3/1, 27/6/91.
207 *Guardian*, 31/3/92.
208 Kusin, V.V., 'The Road to Europe', *RFE Report on Eastern Europe*, 26/10/91.
209 *Romania Libera*, 14/5/91.
210 Peller, S., Reuter, 23/5/91.
211 Tanjug, 25/12/91, SWB EE/1266 C1/10, 31/12/91.
212 Tanjug, 29/1/92, SWB EE/1292.
213 Tanjug, 23/2/92, SWB EE/1313 C1/3 25/2/92.
214 Tanjug, 18/2/92, SWB EE/1309 C18 20/2/92.
215 Tanjug, 18/2/92, SWB EE/1323 C1/6 7/3/92.
216 Croatian Radio, Zagreb, 9/1/92, SWB EE/1277 C1/7, 14/1/92.
217 Tanjug, 4/5/92, SWB EE/1373 C1/14 6/5/92.
218 Tanjug 29/4/92, SWB EE/1370 C1/11 2/5/92.

[219] Croatian Radio, Zagreb, 21/4/92, SWB EE/1363 C1/10, 24/4/92.
[220] Croatian Radio, Zagreb, 28/4/92, SWB EE/1368 C1/7, 30/4/92.
[221] Tanjug, 20/1/92, SWB EE/1284 C1/4, 22/1/92.
[222] Tanjug, 19/12/91, SWB EE/1262 C1/10, 23/12/91.
[223] Croatian Radio, Zagreb, 22/1/92, SWB EE/1288 C1/10, 27/1/92.
[224] MTI 19/2/92, SWB EE/1310 C1/6 21/2/92.
[225] Tanjug, 12/2/92, SWB EE/1305 C1/6, 15/2/92.
[226] Tanjug, 21/2/92, SWB EE/1312 C1/5, 24/2/92.
[227] Tanjug, 1/4/92, SWB EE/1346 C1/11, 3/4/92.
[228] Tanjug, 4/5/92, SWB EE/1373 C1/14, 6/5/92.
[229] Tanjug, 29/4/92, SWB EE/1370 C1/8, 2/5/92.
[230] Croatian Radio, Zagreb, 29/4/92, SWB EE/1370 C1/8, 2/5/92.
[231] Tanjug, 11/1/92, SWB EE/1277 C1/4, 14/1/92.
[232] Tanjug, 20/1/92, SWB EE/1284 C1/3, 22/1/92.
[233] Croatian Radio, Zagreb, 21/1/92, SWB EE/1286, 24/1/92.
[234] Tanjug, 22/1/92, SWB EE/1286 C1/3, 24/1/92.
[235] *Politika Ekspres*, 10/1/92, Tanjug, 10/1/92, SWB EE/1277 C1/4, 14/1/92.
[236] Tanjug, 14/4/92, SWB EE/1359 C1/13, 20/4/92.
[237] Tanjug, 28/4/92, SWB EE/1370 C1/11, 2/5/92.
[238] Newsdesk, BBC World Service, 24/4/92.
[239] Tanner, M., *The Independent*, 21/5/92.
[240] Hungarian Radio, Budapest, 22/10/91, in SWB EE/1210 A2/1, 23/10/91.
[241] Hungarian Radio, Budapest, 29/11/91, in SWB EE/1247 B/9, 5/12/91.
[242] MTI 30/3/92, SWB EE/1348 A2/3 6/4/92.
[243] Interior Minister at press Conference on 16/12/91, MTI 16/12/91 in SWB EE/1259 A2/4, 19/12/91.
[244] RFE WRE, 12/11/91.
[245] RFE WRE, 26/11/91.
[246] Moore, P., 'The Minorities Plight amid Civil War', *RFE* Vol.2, No.50, 13/12/91.
[247] CSTK, 22/1/92, SWB EE/1287 A2/3, 25/1/92.
[248] Tanjug 2/4/92, SWB EE/1353 A1/4 11/4/92.
[249] Morvay, I., State Secretary at the Interior Ministry, Hungarian Radio, Budapest, 3/9/91, in SWB EE/1173 C1/5, 10/9/91.
[250] Hungarian Radio, Budapest, 2/1/92, in SWB EE/1269 i and B/2, 4/2/92.
[251] Hungarian Radio, Budapest, 10/1/92, SWB EE/1281 A1/3, 18/1/92.
[252] Interior Ministry, 10/1/92, MTI 10/1/92, SWB EE/1279 A2/2, 16/2/92.
[253] *Ibid.*
[254] Hungarian Radio, Budapest, 17/3/92, SWB EE/1334 B/6/ 20/3/92.
[255] Interior Ministry, 10/1/92, MTI 10/1/92, SWB EE/1279 A2/2, 16/2/92.
[256] *Ibid.*
[257] *Ibid.*
[258] Prague Home Service, 13/8/90, SWB EE/0844 A2/1, 16/8/90.
[259] *Ibid.*
[260] CSTK 4/3/92, SWB EE/1326 B/7/ 11/3/92.
[261] Figures from PAP in SWB EE/1258 B/12, 12/12/91.
[262] DPA, 12/1/92, SWB EE/1281 A1/1, 18/1/92.
[263] PAP, 8/1/92, SWB EE/1274 B/5, 10/1/92.
[264] *Ibid.*
[265] *Ibid.*

[266] Hungarian Radio, Budapest, 13/1/92 SWB EE/1278 B/5, 15/1/92.
[267] *Ibid.*
[268] Hungarian Radio, Budapest, 2/1/92, SWB EE/1269 i, 4/1/92.
[269] CSTK, 28/11/91, SWB EE/1244 B/3, 2/12/91.
[270] *Gazeta Wyborcza*, 17/12/90 in JPRS-EER-91-013, 31/1/91.
[271] *Przeglad Tygodniowy*, 9/12/90 in JPRS-EER-91-013, 31/1/91.
[272] PAP, 4/4/92, SWB EE/1350 B/10 8/4/92.
[273] PAP, 20/2/92, SWB EE/1312 13/9, 24/2/92.
[274] Interior Ministry, MTI, 8/1/92, SWB EE/1275 B/7, 11/1/92.
[275] *Ibid.*
[276] Hungarian Radio, Budapest, 17/4/92, SWB EE/1360 A2/4, 21/4/92.
[277] Hungarian Radio, Budapest, 14/4/92, SWB EE/1359 B/13, 20/4/92.
[278] Hungarian Radio, Budapest, 10/1/92, SWB EE/1279 B/9, 16/1/92.
[279] *Ibid.*
[280] Hungarian TV, Budapest, 204/2/92, SWB EE/1313 B/7, 25/2/92.
[281] MTI, 2/4/92, SWB EE/1354 B/11, 13/4/92.
[282] Radio Czechoslovakia, 30/12/91, SWB EE/1268 B/6, 3/1/92.
[283] CTSK, 27/12/91, SWB EE/1268 B/6, 3/1/92.
[284] *Rzeczpospolita*, 21/12/90 in JPRS-EER-91-017, 6/2/91.
[285] Chang-Muy, F., 'Greece – A Room and a Job', *Refugees*, No. 84, April 1991.
[286] *Ibid.*
[287] Tanjug, 26/12/91, SWB EE/1266 A1/3, 31/12/91.
[288] SWB EE/1266 A1/1, 31/12/91.
[289] Albanian Radio, Tirana, 14/1/92, SWB EE/1280 ii and A1/1, 17/1/92.
[290] ATA, 3/5/92, and Albanian Radio, Tirana, 4/5/92, SWB EE/1343 A1/2 and A1?3 6/5/92.
[291] Jenny. R., at Bucharest seminar as of note 166.
[292] RFE WRE, 18/8/91.
[293] Ursu, D.V., Romanian Minister of the Interior, Bucharest Conference as of note 166.
[294] DPA, 20/1/92, SWB EE/1287 A1/3, 25/1/92.
[295] Von der Lillie, K.V., Deputy Director of Legal and Consular Affairs at the Austrian Foreign Ministry, at Bucharest Conference as of note 166.
[296] Council of Europe, Parliamentary Assembly, *Recommendation on the Harmonization of National Procedures relating to Asylum*, Recommendation No. R(81) 16, 1981.
[297] ECRE, *Towards Harmonisation of Refugee Policies in Europe? A Contribution to the Discussion*, ECRE, London, October 1988.
[298] Letter to Lord Cockfield, 8/3/88, from the Sub-group on Asylum (European Commission).
[299] Author's interview, Paris 14/7/88, confidential.
[300] EC Commission, *Avant-projet de proposition de Directive du Conseil relative au rapprochement des règles concernant le droit d'asile et le statut des réfugiés*, June 1988, p.31. (Hereafter quoted as *Directive*).
[301] *Accords de Schengen*, Brussels, 21/12/87; *Conclusions de la réunion*, Berlin, 17/12/87, Annexe 1, pp.13-16.
[302] Council of State to Her Majesty the Queen, The Hague, 8/4/91.
[303] *Directive*, Art. 3 to 13, p.39-43.
[304] Schengen, Working Party I and II, Mixed Committee Ad Hoc I and II, 'Border security and border-control', Brussels; Art. 36, 25/4/88.

[305] Schengen Agreement 1990, Chapter 7, Art. 35. 1.2.
[306] *Ibid.*, Chapter 7, Art. 29-4.
[307] Accords de Schengen, Sch/M (87) P and 2. Chapter 2, p.16.
[308] Schengen Agreement 1990, Chapter 6, Art. 26.
[309] *Ibid.*, Chapter 6, Art. 27-1.
[310] Directive, Art. 17, p.65.
[311] *Ibid.*, Art. 14, p.49.
[312] *Ibid.*, Art. 20, 21, p.67-8.
[313] Schengen Agreement 1990, Chapter 7, Art. 38.
[314] *Ibid.*, Chapter 7, Art. 38, Dublin Convention Art. 15.
[315] Schengen, Working Party I and II, Mixed Committee Ad Hoc I and II, *op. cit.*, Art. 28.
[316] Schengen Agreement 1990, Chapter 4, Art. 21, 22.
[317] *Ibid.*
[318] Schengen, Working Party I and II, Mixed Committee Ad Hoc I and II, *op. cit.*, Art. 23.
[319] *Directive*, p.71.
[320] Degimbe, J., *Note à l'attention de M. Braun, Directeur général*, D6III, 24/2/88.
[321] Convention of the Member States of the European Communities on the crossing of their external borders, Art. 8, p.17.
[322] This committee is composed of the Dutch Refugee Council, the Dutch Centre for Migration, the Dutch Section of the International Commission of Jurists, the National Bureau against Racial Discrimination and the Dutch Bar Association.
[323] ECRE, *Report of Bi-annual Participants Meeting*, Geneva, September 1990.
[324] UNHCR, Regional Office in Brussels, *Ratification process of Schengen, UNHCR's position, concerns and recommendations*, 15/10/91.
[325] Rudge, P., ECRE, *Letter*, to Dr Guiseppe Lojacono, Political Coordinator for Community Affairs, 25/9/90 in Report of ECRE, *Participants meeting*, Geneva, 22-23/9/90.
[326] UNHCR, *op. cit.*
[327] EXCOM, *Conclusions*, No.15, 1979.
[328] Council of State to Her Majesty the Queen, The Hague, 8/4/91.
[329] EXCOM, *op. cit.*
[330] Laferrière, F-J., Le droit d'asile et les accords de Schengen, Table Ronde, Paris 25/10/91.
[331] Council of State, *op. cit.*
[332] UNHCR, *op. cit.*
[333] Expert Group meeting on harmonisation efforts in Europe, Minutes of meeting, 10-11/8/92, Appendix 11; Report of ECRE, Participants Meeting, Geneva, 22-23/9/90.
[334] Hunt, J., *Report on Europe of 1992 and refugee policies*, Council of Europe, Parliamentary Assembly, 12/4/91, Doc 6413.
[335] *The Times*, 12/12/92.
[336] Expert Group, *op. cit.*
[337] Council of State, *op. cit.*
[338] Standing Committee of experts on international immigration, refugee and criminal law, *Opinion on ratification of the implementing agreement for the Schengen Agree-ment as recently modified by the agreement of 29 March 1991, between the Schengen countries and the Republic of Poland, with accompanying protocol*, Utrecht, 11/7/91.

[339] Council of Europe, Fourth Conference of European Ministers responsible for Migration Affairs, Conclusions and Resolution adopted by the Conference, Luxembourg, 17-18/9/91.

[340] UNHCR, *op. cit.* and Standing Committee, *op. cit.*

[341] UNHCR, *op. cit.*

[342] Considerations, Conclusions and Recommendations, International Conference on Refugees in the World: The European Community's Response, The Hague at the Upper Chamber of the Dutch Parliament, 7-8/12/89.

[343] Parliamentary Assembly of the Council of Europe, *Recommendation* 953, 1982.

[344] ECRE, *Participants' meeting*, Paris, 23-24/3/90, Appendices.

[345] Council of Europe, Parliamentary Assembly, Recommendation on the arrival of asylum- seekers at European airports, (Recommendation 1163 1991), 23/9/91.

[346] Joly, D., *Harmonising Asylum Policy in Europe*, Policy Papers No.15, CRER, 1988.

[347] *Lawyers Workshop*, ECRE, April 1987.

[348] ECRE, *op. cit.*, p.2.

[349] UNHCR, Working Paper, 1989.

[350] UNHCR, Comments on the Preliminary Draft Proposal for a Council Directive to approximate National Rules on the Grant of Asylum and Refugee Status, 1988, p.3.

[351] Joly, D., *A Refugee Policy for Europe, op. cit.*, p.23.

[352] European Seminar on the Protection of Refugee Children, Swedish Refugee Council with ECRE, 1-8/9/89.

[353] Council of Europe, Fourth Conference of European Ministers, *op. cit.*

[354] MNS, December 1991.

[355] ECRE, Report of Biannual General Meeting, 5-6/10/91.

[356] MNS, November 1991.

[357] *Independent*, 29/6/91.

[358] *Le Monde*, 21/6/91.

[359] *Le Figaro Magazine*, 21/9/91.

[360] *Le Monde*, 6/7/91.

[361] ECRE, Report of Biannual Participants Meeting, 22-23/9/90.

[362] MNS, December 1991.

[363] *Guardian*, 13/7/91.

[364] FORD, G., *Les rapports entre les races à l'intérieur de la Communauté Européenne*, Conférence sur l'égalité des races, Birmingham, 3/12/91.

[365] *Independent*, 19/8/91.

[366] MNS, December 1991.

[367] *L'Humanité*, 21/9/91.

[368] FORD, December 1991.

[369] ECRE, September 1990, *op. cit.*

[370] ECRE, October 1991, *op. cit.*

[371] *Ibid.*

[372] *Ibid.*

[373] Danish Refugee Council, *The effects of carrier sanctions on the asylum system*, Copenhagen, October 1991.

[374] UNHCR, Ratification process of Schengen, 15/10/91, *op. cit.*

[375] Danish Refugee Council, 1991, *op. cit.*

[376] MNS, December 1991.

[377] Joly, *Harmonising asylum policy, op. cit.*
[378] Council of State, *op. cit.*
[379] ECRE, *A refugee policy for Europe*, ECRE, London, September 1987, p.3.
[380] Ministère de l'Intérieur, Service de l'Information et des relations publiques, *Note sur le projet d'application de la Convention de Schengen*, 12/11/91.
[381] UNHCR, Ratification process of Schengen, 15/10/91, *op. cit.*
[382] Expert Group, ECRE, *op. cit.*
[383] Inter-governmental consultations on asylum, refugee and migration policies in Europe, North America and Australia, Strategy Platform, Geneva, September 1991, Report of ECRE Biannual General Meeting, Geneva, 5-6/10/91, Appendix 14.
[384] see Draft Immigration Rules for further information.
[385] Resnick, M., 'Overview on accelerated procedure', *Memorandum*, UNCHR, 23/9/91.
[386] Laferrière, F.J., *op. cit.*
[387] ECRE, Report of Biannual General Meeting, 7-8/3/91.
[388] Danish Refugee Council, 1991, *op. cit.*
[389] ECRE, Participants' meeting, April 1989.
[390] ECRE, March 1991, *op. cit.*
[391] Council of Europe, Recommendation 1163 (91), *op. cit.*
[392] UNHCR, Background note on the safe country concept and refugee status (submitted by the High Commissioner), 3/7/91.
[393] ECRE, October 1991, *op. cit.*
[394] Hailbronner, Dr R., The concept of 'safe country' and expedient asylum procedures, Council of Europe, CAHAR, Strasbourg, 4/9/91.
[395] MNS, December 1991.
[396] UNHCR, *op. cit.*
[397] ECRE, October 1991, *op. cit.*
[398] UNHCR, *op. cit.*
[399] Resnick, 20-23/9/91, *op. cit.*
[400] *Ibid.*
[401] Goodwin-Gill, G., 'Accelerated procedures for the determination of refugee status: possibilities and prospects', unpublished, Geneva, 24/9/91.
[402] Rudge, P., ECRE, *Letter* to Mrs Sadako Ogata, UNHCR, 14/11/91.
[403] Rudge, P., Interview, 5/12/91.
[404] MNS, December 1991.
[405] CDFT, *Letter* to Atalli, 6/9/91.
[406] MNS, November 1991.
[407] MNS, December 1991.
[408] Groupe de Réflexion, Interdépartemental *Stratégie pour la politique des années 90 en matière d'asile et de réfugiés*, Berne, January 1989.
[409] Swedish Ministry of Labour, *A Comprehensive Refugee and Immigration Policy; An outline for an Interdepartmental Study Group*, Working paper for the informal consultation on long-term perspectives and policies, Nyon, 13-14/9/90.
[410] Federal Ministry of Interior, Germany, *Report by the Interministerial Working Group on a 'Refugee Concept'*, Bonn, 25/9/90, V ii 4 936 200 113.
[411] Boddens-Hosang, J.F., *Statement on behalf of the European Community and its member states*, 42nd Session of the Executive Committee of the UNHCR, Geneva, 7/10/91.
[412] Council of Europe, Fourth Conference of European Ministers, *op. cit.*

413 ECRE, Report of Biannual Participants Meeting 22-23/9/90
414 *Ibid.*
415 Federal Ministry of Interior, Germany, *op. cit.*
416 *Ibid.*
415 Section 52, Para 6, of the Aliens Act.
418 ECRE, October 1991, *op. cit.*
419 ECRE, September 1990, *op. cit.*
420 Intergovernmental Consultations Strategy Platform, *op. cit.*
421 ECRE, October 1991, *op. cit.*
422 Theo van Boven,'The significance of 'The Human Dimension' for refugees and asylum- seekers', Oikoumeme Refugees, *Special Issue*, Refugees and asylum seekers in a common European house, August 1991.
423 Hunt, *op. cit.*

SELECT BIBLIOGRAPHY

Governments

FRANCE, REPUBLIC OF, Minisètre de l'Intérieur, Service de l'information et des relations publiques, *Note sur le projet d'application de la Convention de Schengen*, 12/11/91.

GERMANY, FEDERAL REPUBLIC OF, Ministry of the Interior, *Report by the Interministerial Working Group on a 'Refugee Concept'*, Vii 4 936 200 113, Bonn, 25/9/90.

NETHERLANDS, KINGDOM OF, *Council of State to Her Majesty the Queen*, The Hague, 8/4/91.

SWITZERLAND, CONFEDERATION OF, Groupe de Réflexion Interdépartemental, *Stratégie pour la politique des années 90 en matiere d'asile et de réfugiés*, Berne, January 1989.

SWEDEN, KINGDOM OF, Swedish Ministry of Labour, A comprehensive refugee and immigration policy Directives for a government committee August 1990, Working paper for the informal consultation on long-term perspectives and policies, Nyon, 13-14/9/90.

Council of Europe

BÖHM, Mr, Council of Europe, Parliamentary Assembly, *Report on living and working conditions of refugees and asylum-seekers*, Doc 5380, 26/3/85.

COUNCIL OF EUROPE, Parliamentary Assembly, 37th ordinary session, Recommendation 1016 (1985) on living and working conditions of refugees and asylum-seekers.

COUNCIL OF EUROPE, Parliamentary Assembly, 40th ordinary session, Recommendation 1088 (1988) on the right to territorial asylum.

COUNCIL OF EUROPE, Ad Hoc Committee of Experts on the Legal Aspects of Territorial Asylum, Refugees and Stateless Persons (CAHAR), Strasbourg, 25/1/89, Draft agreement on responsibility for examining asylum requests.

COUNCIL OF EUROPE, Committee of Experts for the promotion of education and information in the field of human rights, Proceedings of the Colloquy on human rights without frontiers, Strasbourg, 30/11-1/12/89.

COUNCIL OF EUROPE, Fourth conference of European Ministers responsible for Migration Affairs, Conclusions and resolution adopted by the conference, Luxembourg, 17-18/9/91.

COUNCIL OF EUROPE, Parliamentary Assembly, Recommendation 1163 (1991) (1) on the arrival of asylum-seekers at European airports, 23/9/91.

HAILBRONNER, Dr R., *The concept of 'safe country' and expedient asylum procedures*, Council of Europe, CAHAR, Strasbourg, 4/9/91.

OFFENBECK, Mme., Council of Europe Parliamentary Assembly, *Report on the right to territorial asylum*, Doc 5930, 23/8/88.

HUNT, J., *Report on Europe of 1992 and Refugee Policies*, Council of Europe, Parliamentary Assembly, Doc 6413, 12/4/91.

MACKIE, Lord of Benshie, (MEP), Council of Europe, Parliamentary Assembly, *Report on the arrival of asylum-seekers at European airports*, 12/9/91.

SALT, J., 'Current and future international migration trends affecting Europe, Council of Europe, Fourth conference of European ministers responsible for migration affairs, Luxembourg 17- 18/9/91.

European Communities

BODDENS-HOSANG, J.F., *Statement on behalf of the European Community and its member states*, 42nd Session of the Executive Committee of the UNHCR, Geneva, 7/10/91.

EUROPEAN COMMISSION, *Text F Communication to the Parliament and Council on Immigration*, Document 0/91/126, Brussels, 29/4/90.

Inter-governmental documents

AD HOC GROUP ON IMMIGRATION, Convention of the Member States of the European Communities on the crossing of their external borders, Brussels, 24/6/91.

EXPERT GROUP MEETING ON HARMONISATION EFFORTS IN EUROPE, Minutes of meeting, (Appendix 11), 10-11/8/91.

INTER-GOVERNMENTAL CONSULTATIONS ON ASYLUM, REFUGEE AND MIGRATION POLICIES IN EUROPE, NORTH AMERICA AND AUSTRALIA, *Strategy Platform*, (Appendix 14), Geneva, September 1991.

MINISTERIAL CONFERENCE on the movements of persons from Eastern and Central Europe, *Final communiqué* (Appendix 13), 24-25/1/91.

UNHCR

ARNIM, Ruprecht von, *Présentation du Délégué régional auprès des pays du Bénélux et des institutions européennes, lors de la réunion du Groupe Central des négociations de Schengen*, 25/10/91.

RESNICK, M., 'Overview on accelerated procedure', *Memorandum*, UNHCR, 23/9/91.

UNHCR, *UNHCR activities financed by voluntary funds: Report for 1990-91 and proposed programmes and budget for 1992, Part III Europe and North America*, Geneva, 19/8/91.

UNHCR, *Background note on the safe country concept and refugee status* (submitted by the High Commissioner), 3/7/91.

UNHCR, Regional Office in Brussels, *Ratification process of Schengen UNHCR's position, concerns and recommendations*, 15/10/91.

Non-Government Organizations
AMNESTY INTERNATIONAL, *Amnesty International's Concerns in Western Europe*, October 1986-March 1987, SF 87 10 110, EUR 03/01/87, April 1987.
AMNESTY INTERNATIONAL, *Harmonisation of Asylum Policy in Europe: Amnesty International's Concerns*, London, April 1990.
AMNESTY INTERNATIONAL (French section), *Les sanctions aux transporteurs, Des difficultés d'accès au territoire*, Paris, 20/11/91.
CONFERENCE OF EUROPEAN CHURCHES, *To the heads of state and of government of the Signatory States of the Helsinki Final Act*, 2/11/90.
DANISH REFUGEE COUNCIL, *The role of airline companies in the asylum procedure*, Copenhagen, July 1988.
DANISH REFUGEE COUNCIL, *The effects of carrier sanctions on the asylum system*, Copenhagen, October 1991.
DUTCH REFUGEE COUNCIL and NETHERLANDS INSTITUTE FOR HUMAN RIGHTS, *Refugees in the World: the European Community's Response* – Report of the International Conference, SIM Special no.10, Joint publication of SIM and the Dutch Refugee Council, Utrecht, December 1990.
EUROPEAN CONSULTATION ON REFUGEES AND EXILES (ECRE), *Refugee Policy in a Unifying Europe*, Report of an ECRE Seminar held in Ziest, 1989.
ECRE, *Fair and efficient procedures for determining refugee status*, London, October 1990.
ECRE, *Asile en Europe*, Paris, 1990.
INFORMAL MEETING OF WORKING GROUP ON UNDOCUMENTED ASYLUM SEEKERS, *Inter-governmental Consultations on asylum and refugee policies*, (Appendix 12), Geneva, 27-28/8/90.
INTERNATIONAL SOCIAL SERVICE, *Unaccompanied Refugee Children in Europe Experience with Protection Placement and Education.*
NORWEGIAN ORGANIZATION FOR ASYLUM SEEKERS (NOAS), *A wall around Europe – consequences for Norway*, n.d.
PERMANENT COMMITTEE OF EXPERTS ON INTERNATIONAL ALIEN, REFUGEE AND CRIMINAL LAW POLICY, Report (Committee established by the Dutch Refugee Council, the Dutch Centre for Migration, the Dutch Section of the International Commission of Jurists, the National Bureau against Racial Discrimination and the Dutch Bar Association). *A secret text for a convention on asylum-seekers by the twelve EC countries has almost reached official completion; will the Schengen Agreement also come up for discussion again?*
US COMMITTEE FOR REFUGEES, *World Refugee Survey*, Washington, (published annually).

Books

COHEN, R., and JOLY, D., (Eds), *Reluctant Hosts: Europe and its Refugees*, Gower, Aldershot, 1989.

GOODWIN-GILL, G.S., *The refugee in international law*, Clarendon Press, Oxford, 1983.

INDEPENDENT COMMISSION ON INTERNATIONAL HUMANITARIAN ISSUES, *Refugees: the Dynamics of Displacement*, Zed Books, London, 1987.

MARRUS, M.R., *The Unwanted: European Refugees in the twentieth century*, OUP, New York, 1985.

ZARJEVSKI, M., *A Future Preserved: International assistance to refugees*, Pergamon Press/UNHCR, Oxford, 1988.

ZOLBERG, A., et. al., *Escape from Violence: Conflict and the Refugee Crisis in the Developing World*, OUP, Oxford, 1989.

Articles and Journals

GALLAGHER, D., *The Era of Refugees: The Evolution of the International Refugee System*, Refugee Policy Group, Washington 1989,

LAFERRIERE, F-J., *Le droit d'asile et les accord de Schengen*, Table Ronde, Paris, 25/10/91.

LOESCHER, G., 'The European Community and refugees' in *International Affairs*, Royal Institute of International Affairs, Vol 65, Part 4, London, 1989.

MELANDER, G., *The two refugee definitions*, Report No. 4, Raoul Wallenberg Institute, Lund, 1987.

OIKOUMENE REFUGEES, *Special Issue, Refugees and asylum-seekers, a common European house*, August 1991.

RUDGE, P., *Refugee policy to 1992 and beyond*, Intervention at the commemoration of the 40th anniversary of the Geneva Convention relating to the status of refugees, June 1991.

RUDGE, P., *Into the 1990s*, The Refugee Council, London, 1990.

Other documents

DARLING, A., M.P., *Completion of the Single Market 1992, Freedom of Movement and Asylum*, November 1991.

FORD, G., *Les rapports entre les races à l'intérieur de la Communauté Européenne*, Conférence sur l'égalité des races, Birmingham 3/12/91.

GOODWIN-GILL, G., *Accelerated procedures for the determination of refugee status: possibilities and prospects*, unpublished, Geneva, 24/9/91.

STANDING COMMITTEE OF EXPERTS ON INTERNATIONAL IMMIGRATION, REFUGEE AND CRIMINAL LAW, *Opinion on ratification of the implementing agreement for the Schengen Agreement as recently modified by the agreement of March 29, 1991, between the Schengen countries and the republic of Poland, with accompanying protocol Utrecht*, 11/7/91.

INDEX